First Steps
in Inner Development

First Steps

in Inner Development

Rudolf Steiner

✑ Anthroposophic Press

Published by Anthroposophic Press
3390 Route 9, Hudson, NY 12534
www.anthropress.org

"The Inner Life" [Vom inneren Leben], lecture by Rudolf Steiner in Berlin, December 15, 1904, is included in *Urspung und Ziel des Menschen* (volume 53 of the Bibliographic Survey, 1981). It was translated from the German original by Catherine Creeger. Copyright © 1999 by Anthroposophic Press, Inc.

"The Path" [Innere Entwickelung], lecture in Berlin, December 7, 1905, is included in *Die Welträtsel und die Anthroposophie* (volume 54 of the Bibliographic Survey, 1983). It was translated from the German original by Catherine Creeger. Copyright © 1999 by Anthroposophic Press, Inc.

"First Steps" [Innere Entwickelung], given in Berlin, April 19, 1906, is included in *Die Welträtsel und die Anthroposophie* (volume 54 of the Bibliographic Survey, 1983). It was translated from the German original by Catherine Creeger. Copyright © 1999 by Anthroposophic Press, Inc.

"The Way to Inner Development" (extracts) [Die orientalische und die christliche Schulung], given in Stuttgart, September 3, 1906, is included in *Vor dem Tore der Theosophie* (volume 95 in the Bibliographic Survey, 1990). The original translation was revised by "E. H. G." from which extracts have been edited against the German for this volume by Christopher Bamford. Copyright © 1999 by Anthroposophic Press, Inc.

"How Does the Soul Discover Its True Being?" [Wie findet die Seele ihre wahre Wesenheit?], given in *Das Goethenum*, 1945, vol. 24, no. 16–22 (Freiburg, 1953) translated from the German original by Catherine Creeger. Copyright © 1999 by Anthroposophic Press, Inc.

Library of Congress Cataloging-in-Publication Data

Steiner, Rudolf, 1861–1925.
    [Lectures. English. Selections]
    First steps in inner developemnt / Rudolf Steiner.
      p. cm.
    Includes bibliographical references
    Contents: The inner life — The path — Ways to inner development (extracts) — How does the soul find its true being?
      ISBN 0-88010-464-3 (paper)
      1. Spiritual life—Anthroposophy. I. Title.
    BP595.S894L4213   1999
    299'.935--dc21   99-36521
                                           CIP

10 9 8 7 6 5 4 3 2 1

Printed in the United States of America

Contents

Introduction

It is one of the tragedies of our time that the sheer vastness of Rudolf Steiner's accomplishments and gifts to humanity has served to obscure his greatness and relevance. He was a "Renaissance figure," so multifaceted a genius in so many different fields, that most people have found it easier to ignore him than to struggle to fit him into one of the categories we usually use to domesticate revolutionary thinkers and remove their sting. Steiner (1861-1925) was so many things—to name only a few: a philosopher, a scientist, an educator, a social thinker, an artist, a Christian mystic, a full-consciousness clairvoyant and trained scientist of the invisible, a spiritual initiate and teacher—that ignoring him has seemed the best policy. For this reason, he has been called "the best-kept secret of the twentieth century."

This little book on "inner development," however, should put no one off. It calls out *not* to be ignored, for it shows Rudolf Steiner as a spiritual teacher of the utmost seriousness, compassion, and wisdom. Anyone who wishes to unfold their own capacities of soul and spirit will be able to draw encouragement and advice from it. At the same time, those already on a path—no matter which—will discover here nuances and "professional tips" of untold usefulness.

Rudolf Steiner did not assume the mantle of teacher until his forty-first year. He spent the first part of his life mastering the very essence of modern consciousness by extensive study and experience in the fields of philosophy (especially epistemology, the study of how we *know*), science, mathematics, literature, and art. Though springing from humble origins, Steiner nevertheless became a man of letters, an independent scholar and researcher, well known for his work with the revolutionary natural science of the great German poet Goethe, as well as for his work on Nietzsche and his original contributions to philosophy. Around the turn of the century, approaching his fortieth year, he moved to Berlin, then the cultural capital of Central Europe, to edit a literary magazine and take part in the new Workers Education movement. But greater things awaited him.

Steiner was born a clairvoyant and his world-mission was never anything other than spiritual. While pursuing his philosophical, scientific, and academic careers, he never deviated from his devotion to the spiritual world. He always saw his task as esoteric—though he recognized that it was not yet time to acknowledge this publicly. Evidence of this esoteric life may be seen in his encountering, first, a wise healer, nature-knower, and gatherer of herbs, Felix Kogutzki, and then, following this, a further encounter with a mysterious being he calls M. (the Master)—thought by some to be Christian Rosenkreutz. Around the same time (the 1880s), he became acquainted with the Theosophical movement—but this, at that time, as he says, had no "*outward* consequence." It was not until the turn of the century that the actual call came to assume his true role. In 1902 he helped establish the German Section of the Theosophical Society and took on the task of general secretary. This was not a bureaucratic position. He took on the leadership of the Esoteric Section and did not shirk the responsibilities of becoming a spiritual teacher in a mode appropriate to our time.

Many books and lectures attest to his mastery in the field of inner development. Here we have gathered a few of the key lectures in which he lays down the essentials of the path as he knew it. Deceptively simple, and not at all dated, these lectures are pure gold.

Christopher Bamford

1. THE INNER LIFE

Berlin

DECEMBER 15, 1904

In my lectures on basic spiritual scientific concepts, I took the liberty of sketching for you the so-called three worlds—the physical world, the soul world, and the spiritual world—and the essential nature of the human being. In the new year, my task will be to elaborate on the most important spiritual scientific insights into the origins of the human being, as well as those of the Earth and other heavenly bodies, in order to provide a broader view of the image of the world that theosophy can outline for us.

Today, however, I would like to give a few indications on how inner development must proceed if we want to become personally convinced of the truths proclaimed by the spiritual scientific worldview. Please consider that we need to distinguish between the education of the human soul and spirit that leads to personal understanding of the truths, insights, and experiences proclaimed by spiritual scientists, and a second level of training, which makes it possible to acquire such knowledge and experiences for ourselves. The elementary level of training enables us to affirm the statements of experienced mystics, to say "I understand this; I can think it and feel it for myself and even acknowledge its truth within certain limits." We need to distinguish, however, between this elementary level and a higher level that makes us capable of directly experiencing the world of soul or spirit for ourselves. Today, we will consider the first level. The second level has to do with clairvoyance as such, and to the extent that it is possible to comment publicly on this subject, we will consider it in a later lecture.[1]

The question we will consider today is how to come to a personal understanding of spiritual scientific truths. Please do not think that I can provide more than a few suggestions, because the human soul and spirit must undergo a long and comprehensive schooling in order to achieve this understanding to any extent. A long, long period of inner study is needed, and its many detailed requirements cannot even be touched upon in one short lecture. What I can tell you today relates to personal instruction in this field in the same sense that a description of a microscope or telescope relates to actually learning to use the instrument in a laboratory or observatory.

We must note, first of all, that before true instruction can occur in this field most people need a personal teacher. It may seem to many of you that individuals should be able to develop inner soul capacities such as spiritual sight by themselves through individual experimentation, and it may be distressing to hear that direct personal guidance is needed in this important area of life. Only the quality of this direct guidance, however, adequately guarantees that the student will not become dependent in any way on anyone else. No one honors and respects what we call human dignity and self-esteem more highly than esoteric teachers do. Instructors of mystical and spiritual scientific development offer no more than advice. The highest teachers in these fields have always given nothing but advice and suggestions. It is entirely up to the individual to decide to what extent to follow them, or not. It is up to

---

1. It is unclear which lectures this and a later comment refer to.

us as individuals to set tasks for our own soul and spirit. Human freedom is held in such high esteem that the teacher will give only advice and suggestions. These reservations apply to everything that can be said on this subject.

You must also realize that the most important aspect of this training has nothing to do with specific outer conditions, nor does it require specific external measures. Rather, it is a very intimate instruction of the human soul. All of its important steps take place deep within the individual. The transformation need not be noticeable even to the person's closest friend. Mystics—that is, people aspiring to an understanding of the world of soul and spirit—are educated in silence, peace, and seclusion. It must be emphasized repeatedly that esoteric students are not required to make any changes at all in their daily occupation, nor should they neglect or withdraw from their daily responsibilities simply because they believe it necessary to devote a specific period of time to mystical self-education. On the contrary, if they neglect their responsibilities and become poor citizens and poor members of human society as a consequence of attempting to acquire insight into higher worlds, they will soon be convinced that this is the least successful means of accomplishing anything in this field.

Inner training takes place in complete inner peace, silently rather than tumultuously. Let me emphasize that I am not giving any "special" indications; I am simply describing a path that demands one thing, namely, patience, which is also the one quality without which personal higher experience can never be acquired. As a rule, anyone who lacks steadfastness and patience, anyone who cannot persist in silently obeying the relevant inner rules again and again, will accomplish nothing. There is only one possible way of achieving anything without following these rules, and it applies only to those who are highly advanced in terms of the development of their essential human nature. For those who have already achieved a certain level of clairvoyance in an earlier life, the way is much shorter and completely different. The person entrusted with providing the appropriate guidance will soon notice this situation and will then need only to eliminate the relevant obstacles to progress.

As a general rule, it is not advisable to attempt mystical development without personal guidance, because the right way to achieve such development is different for almost every individual. Furthermore, the person who provides guidance must know the pupil very well—not in the ordinary sense of the word, but in the spiritual sense. The esoteric teacher need not know anything about the pupil's occupation, lifestyle, family members, or experiences. All that is required is an intimate knowledge of the pupil's current level of soul and spirit. (Today we cannot discuss how an esoteric teacher acquires such knowledge; that will be presented in lectures on clairvoyance.) Furthermore, inner development is linked to specific consequences, and anyone who sets out on this path must expect very specific qualities—the "symptoms" of inner development—to appear within one's essential nature. These qualities are signs of inner development and must be observed carefully. The esoteric teacher must know how to interpret these symptoms if the student's development is to proceed in the right way.

The development of the inner human being is a birth—a birth of soul and spirit—not in a merely metaphorical or figurative sense, but in the truest, most factual sense of the word. Even in this realm, birth has consequences, and the esoteric teacher must know how to deal with them.

I needed to say all this as an introduction. At this point, you yourselves are more or less able to ask the questions that people typically have when they first hear about the basic teachings of spiritual science—about reincarnation, the many past and future incarnations of the human soul in a body, and about karma, the doctrine of compensatory justice. You will ask how to acquire a personal understanding of these teachings. This is the great question that arises for each individual. All those who have truly submitted to the appropriate exercises experience that there is only one golden rule that must be followed in order to arrive at such an understanding. This is the easiest way in the world; no one who follows it is incapable of understanding reincarnation and karma. And yet, like Goethe, we might say, "Sure, it's easy, but this easy is hard,"[2] because very few people find the resolve, steadfastness, and patience to work out the very specific processes of soul and spirit needed for this understanding. This golden rule is: When you live as if reincarnation and karma were truths, they will become truths for you. It may seem as if this is supposed to be achieved through some sort of autosuggestion, but this is not the case. You are familiar with the ouroboros, the mystical symbol of the serpent biting its own tail. This symbol has many deep meanings, one of which is expressed in this golden rule.

You can see that, in a certain sense, the prerequisite to understanding consumes itself just like the circling snake. How can we make this happen? If reincarnation is a fact, then certain efforts people make will inevitably affect their souls, and these effects will later become an integral part of their character. One of the great laws that human beings have postulated and that individuals must test on themselves is expressed in an Indian work in these words: What you think today, you will become tomorrow. Those who believe in reincarnation must realize that any quality they develop in themselves, any notion they impress upon themselves by entertaining it over and over again, becomes permanent in their soul, where it will have to appear repeatedly.

Thus it is most important for those attempting mystical development to experiment with eliminating habits and inclinations and acquiring new ones. Simply entertaining the appropriate thoughts allows the corresponding inclinations, virtues, or qualities to follow until they are so firmly ensconced that we become capable of transforming our own soul through acts of will. We must accomplish this through experimentation, just as a chemical experiment is carried out. You will not be able to make much of the truths of reincarnation and karma if you have never attempted

---

2. *Faust* 2, act 1.

to transform your own soul, never summoned up the resolve to develop the qualities of endurance, steadfastness, and calm, logical thinking and stuck to it. Even when a week has gone by with no sign of success, you must persevere and spend a month, a year, or even a decade on the effort.

This is the inner route the soul must follow. It must be able to incorporate new qualities, thoughts, and inclinations. The individual must be capable of developing completely new habits over a certain period of time, simply by exercising personal will. For example, through personal resolve rather than external duress, a careless person must develop the habit of being precise and exact. This exercise is especially effective when we apply it to minor qualities. The more clearly we change, the more certainly we will come to true understanding in this area. As soon as we are able to observe our own gestures, facial expressions, or other insignificant habits objectively, as if observing them in someone else, and as soon as we are able to use the strength of our will to replace these habits with ones we choose and incorporate into ourselves, we are well on the way to acquiring a personal understanding of the great law of reincarnation. An experienced chemist can supply indications of what is going on in the laboratory. Similarly, those who have performed such experiments on their own souls will also be able to provide certain suggestions that have been personally tested. The greatest good is achieved through small transformations.

We learn to understand karma, the great law of just compensation, by living as if it were indeed a truth. Whenever you are affected by pain, accident, or the like, try again and again to entertain the idea that your misfortune did not come into the world through some miracle. It must have a cause, which, however, you need not investigate. Only those who have a real overview of karma will be able to see the cause of a pain, a stroke of luck, and so forth. You yourself must simply submit to the feeling that such an event, whether pain or pleasure, must have a cause, which will also be the cause of events in the future.

If you imbue yourself with this feeling and assume that karma is indeed a truth as you observe your life and all its events that storm in from outside, you will find that karma becomes comprehensible. If you are able to stop your anger when misfortune strikes and imagine that the event causing your anger, like a stone that begins to roll when it is kicked, must also have a cause and run its course according to some lawful process in the world, you will come to an understanding of karma. You understand karma if you look at life in this way. This is as certain as the fact that you will wake up tomorrow morning—assuming that nothing changes and you remain healthy.

These ways of looking at life are the two prerequisites for anyone who chooses to undertake spiritual training. It is not necessary to submit immediately to these thoughts as if they were truths. We must leave it free and open—perhaps they are true, perhaps not. Neither doubt nor superstition is allowed, however, because these are the most significant obstacles. Only when we are ready to observe life in this way are we ready to receive instruction in mysticism.

And there is still a third prerequisite. No esoteric teacher will ever agree to instruct someone who is possessed by superstition or prejudice of the crudest sort, or who tends to make irrational judgments or succumb to illusion. The golden rule is that an individual, before achieving the first level of inner development, must become free of all illusory thoughts and superstitions and of any possibility of mistaking illusion for reality. Above all, an esoteric student must be rational and submit only to the rigorous consequences of his or her thoughts and observations. If you submit to prejudice or superstition in sensory perceptible reality, you will soon be corrected. But if you fantasize instead of thinking logically, the correction is not so easy. That is why you must be completely secure in your thought life and exercise strict control over your thoughts before entering the worlds of soul and spirit. Anyone who tends toward fantasy, superstition, and illusions is unsuited to embark on the elementary level of spiritual training.

Such a person may well claim to be free of fantasy, superstition, and illusion, but self-deception is easy in such cases. Freedom from prejudice, fantasy, illusion, and superstition must be acquired through strict self-discipline. These qualities are not easy for everyone to acquire. Just think of how most people jump around in their mental activity like will-o'-the-wisps and cannot strictly control their thoughts through personal strength of will.

Now let us consider the character of our ordinary life. We cannot always remain free of outer impressions, so we need to set aside a brief period every day. The short time we can take without conflicting with our responsibilities is sufficient, even if it is only five minutes or less. During this time, however, we must be able to tear ourselves away from everything that our sense impressions offer us, from everything we take in through our eyes, ears, and sense of touch. For a time we must become blind and deaf to our surroundings. Everything that comes toward us from outside links us to the sensory world and to daily life. All of that must fall silent for a while; complete inner peace must descend. Once we accomplish this inner peace, this stripping off of all sensory impressions, we must also silence all recollection of past sensory impressions. Just think how everything I have just listed binds us to time and space and to everything that comes into being and passes away. Try testing this briefly. Check the thought that was going through your head a minute ago—was it related to something transitory? Such thoughts are not suited to inner development.

All thoughts that link us to the finite and transitory must fall silent. When this peace has been produced in the soul, when the time, race, nationality, and century that we are embedded in have been overcome, and inner silence has descended for a time, the soul begins to speak of its own accord. This does not happen immediately. First we must bring the soul to the point of speaking, and there are ways and means of doing so.

We must submit to thoughts, images, and sensations that originate in eternity rather than in the temporal. It is not enough that they were true a hundred years ago, or that they are true for today, yesterday, and tomorrow. They must be true forever. You will find such thoughts in the various religious books of all peoples—in the Bhagavad Gita, the song of human perfection, for example, and also in the New and Old Testaments, especially in the Gospel according to John, from chapter thirteen on. Thoughts that are particularly effective for people who belong to the theosophical movement are provided in the booklet *Light on the Path*, especially in the first four sentences.[3] These four sentences, which are engraved on the interior walls of every temple of initiation, are not dependent on time and space. They do not belong to an individual, a family, a century, or a generation; they extend throughout evolution. They were true thousands of years ago and will be true for thousands of years to come. They awaken forces slumbering within us and draw them up from within us. Admittedly, this must be done in the right way. It is not enough to think that we understand such a sentence. We must let it come alive within us. We must submit to it totally, allowing all its power to radiate within us. We must learn to love the sentence. When we believe we have understood it, that simply means the time has come to allow it to shine within us again and again. Our intellectual understanding of the sentence is not the point; the point is to love its spiritual truth. The more we love such inner truths and feel this love streaming through us, the more the power of inner sight awakens in us. If we remain involved with such a sentence not only for a day or two but for weeks, months, and years, it will awaken soul forces within us. This is followed by another illumination at a very specific moment.

---

3. "Before the eyes can see, they must be incapable of tears. Before the ear can hear, it must have lost its sensitiveness. Before the voice can speak in the presence of the Masters, it must have lost the power to wound. Before the soul can stand in the presence of the Masters, its feet must be washed in the blood of the heart." Steiner explains the significance of these four sentences in his "Exegesis to *Light on the Path*," in *From the History and Contents of the First Section of the Esoteric School 1904–1914*, p. 425–434.

Those who proclaim spiritual scientific truths on the basis of personal experience are aware of this inner, contemplative life. These truths are the same today and tomorrow. They are part of a grand spiritual scientific image of the world that their proclaimers perceive with the inner power of their spirits and souls. In order to investigate these truths, they turn their gaze toward the worlds of soul and spirit, away from Earth and toward the heavenly bodies. Their ability to do so would soon die away, however, if it were not nourished each morning. That is the secret of esoteric researchers. Each morning, they review the grand image of the cosmos and humanity that they have allowed to pass before their souls hundreds and hundreds of times before. The point is not that they understand everything about this image, but that they learn to love it more and more by performing a religious ritual every morning in which they look up to the divine spirits. They have learned to review the entire image in a few minutes and are filled with gratitude for what their souls have received from it. Without traveling this path of reverence, it is not possible to achieve the clarity that must shape the words of spiritual teachers who are truly called upon to speak about the truths of mysticism, theosophy, and spiritual science.

This is how spiritual researchers do it, and this is what everyone must do: We begin in the simplest, most elementary way in order to reach an understanding of these teachings. Human nature and the nature of cosmic beings are profound, infinitely profound. Nothing is achieved in this domain except through patience, endurance, and love for the cosmic powers. In the inner world, these qualities are forces, forces as powerful as electricity in the outer world. They are not only moral but also cognitive forces.

Once esoteric students have practiced allowing such truths to dwell in them for a time, and once they accept these truths with gratitude toward those who reveal them, a moment comes to each one who has allowed peace and stillness to develop in his or her soul. This is the moment when the soul itself begins to speak, when the person's inner being begins to perceive great eternal truths. Then suddenly the surrounding world is illuminated with colors never before seen and resounds with sounds not previously heard. The world glows with a new light; new sounds and words become perceptible. This new light shines from the soul world, and the newly audible sounds resound from the spirit world. It is characteristic of these worlds that the soul world is seen, the spirit world heard.

I have only been able to sketch in broad strokes how inner development comes about, and how it is experienced; there are many individual rules to obey if you yourself want to attempt development in this domain. These individual rules are meant to be followed precisely, just as chemists must measure tiny amounts of substances and use the finest instruments to measure what they need to make a particular compound. A full description of these rules, to the extent that they can be made public, can be found in my book *How to Know Higher Worlds* [see bibliography]. These further rules offer guidance on how we must travel this path of knowledge. They, too, demand extreme inward patience and endurance.

In earlier times, these rules were never made public. Please be clear that today, as in the past, esoteric instruction is conducted only in esoteric schools, because it is a very intimate form of instruction from person to person. It is of no use to seek guidance in the fragments you read or hear about and to experiment with them. As a rule, that is completely useless. Any guidance you can gain from one perspective or another—and there are even businesses that advertise such guidance—is nothing more than tiny fragments of the great book of esoteric training. Anyone who makes use of them must realize the dangers involved. It is by no means advisable to approach matters of inner soul transformation, the soul's greatest and most significant aspect, in a business context. Anything in this domain that is advertised for sale will prove to be not only valueless but possibly also dangerous to you. I need to make this statement because people are being confronted with so much of this. The rules laid out in *How to Know Higher Worlds* originate in age-old traditions. The Masters of

Wisdom have given permission for such rules to be published in order to counter advances that are being made to people from all sides and to contrast such suggestions with an image of the truth. Only a few details can be published, however; publication of the rest is prohibited. What is most important must be conveyed orally. What you can find in *How to Know Higher Worlds*, unlike much that is made public, is harmless. The exercises presented there will cause no harm, even when they are not carried out with patience and steadfastness. No one can suffer any harm from these exercises. I needed to say this because I have been asked why some of these rules have been communicated recently.

The point I want to make here is that, in order to become conscious in the soul world, you need the appropriate organs of perception, just as you do in the sensory perceptible world. Just as your body has eyes and ears, your soul and spirit must possess organs for perceiving soul light and spirit sound. Those who are experienced and can perceive in this domain see these organs beginning to emerge, as if in a cloud of light, in the aura of a person undergoing inner development. In an undeveloped individual, the aura is shaped like a cloud that floats over the physical body when that person is asleep and the astral body separates from the physical body. Under these circumstances, the astral body becomes visible in the form of two intertwined spirals, like rings of smoke. They intertwine and continue to spiral until they become indistinct. Two such intertwined rings constitute the aura of people who are asleep. As individuals develop esoterically, their auras become increasingly defined. The ends of the spirals that spin out into the distance disappear, and the two intertwining formations begin to form organs. To an ever greater extent, they become a definite, enclosed formation with very specific organs. The organs that appear in the aura are known as chakras. They are the sense organs of the soul and do not develop under any other conditions. They are very delicate formations that must be carefully tended. Anyone who neglects their care will never really enjoy soul vision.

The eye of the soul must be cultivated by suppressing all negative sensations and feelings. The chakras cannot emerge in an individual who flies into a rage at any opportunity. Equanimity and patience are needed, because anger and rage prevent the emergence of the soul organs, as do hastiness and nervousness.

Furthermore, it is necessary to abandon a quality that is extremely difficult to eliminate in our culture, namely, the desire to constantly experience the latest news. This desire has a great impact on the eyes of the soul. People who can't get to the newspaper quickly enough, who must immediately pass the latest story on to someone else as soon as they've learned about it, or who cannot see or hear anything and keep it to themselves, can never develop their souls.

It is also necessary to learn to assess our fellow human beings in a very specific way, without criticism. This is very difficult. We need understanding rather than criticism. If you immediately confront your fellow human beings with your own criticism, it suppresses your soul's development. We must first listen to the other person. Such listening is an extremely effective means of developing the eyes of the soul. Those who reach a higher level on this path owe their advancement to having given up the habit of criticizing and judging everything. How can we see into another person's soul? We should understand criminals rather than condemning them; we should understand the criminal as well as the saint. Every human being needs understanding, and understanding is a higher, esoteric form of listening. Esoteric, or occult, powers become possible for people who are firmly resolved not to assess either their fellow human beings or anything else on the basis of their own personal judgment, opinions, or prejudices; instead, they allow people and events to work on them in silence. Every moment in which we refrain from some bad thought about a fellow human being is a moment gained.

The wisest person can learn from a child, and the simplest person may say, "What's that child chattering on about? I know it all much better." Such a person, however, may also say, "What is that wise person chattering on about? What good is it to me?" Only when we listen to a child's stammering as if it were a revelation do we create strength in ourselves that wells up out of the soul.

We cannot expect the eyes of the soul to develop overnight. When we combat rage, anger, curiosity, and so forth, we are initially only doing away with obstacles that formerly obstructed the soul like dams. This has to be done over and over again, with ever-renewed efforts. Esotericists can assess how the delicate soul organs are developing. When our human words have forgotten how to wound—when they are no longer cutting and pointed but have become gentle enough to understand a fellow human being— the chakra in the area of the larynx awakens. Individuals must work for a long time, however, before they are able to perceive this organ in themselves. In the physical human being, nature shaped the location of the eye first, and then the beginnings of a lens, and so the physical eye evolved very slowly and gradually over the course of millions of years. The eye of the soul does not take that long to develop. For some people, it takes just a few months; for others, a longer period of time. Patience is needed, but eventually the moment comes for each one of us when this delicate structure begins to see. Then we must continue these exercises in the right way, particularly if we want to develop certain virtues that occasionally permit the life of the person we are considering to be reflected in ourselves. Developing three virtues in particular is almost enough to make a person a seer if these virtues are practiced with appropriate intensity. These virtues are: self-confidence linked with humility, self-control with gentleness, and presence of mind with steadfastness. These are the great levers in developing our spiritual organs. The three primary virtues, however, lead to terrible vices if they are not coupled with the three other virtues of humility, gentleness, and steadfastness.

These are suggestions that can be given at present. I have selected examples of how esoteric students go through the three stages we call preparation (or catharsis), illumination, and initiation, which are the same as the three levels in an esoteric school.

The preparation stage equips us in such a way that the delicate soul organs can appear. Through illumination, we acquire the ability to see in the domain of the soul; thorough initiation, we develop the faculty of self-expression in the spiritual realm. What I have described today may seem difficult to many of you. In fact, it is easy, but it is, indeed, also a case of an easy thing being difficult.

Anyone can set out on the esoteric path; it is closed to no one. The mysteries are present in the breast of each human being. All that is required is serious inner work and the possibility to free ourselves of all the obstacles that block this subtle inner life. We must realize that the world's greatest and most distant aspects are revealed to us in the most intimate of ways. Humanity's wisest members had no other means of attaining great truths than the path described here. They achieved these truths because they discovered the path within themselves, because they knew that they had to practice patience and steadfastness in carrying out these routines. When people immerse themselves in their inner being in this way, when they lift themselves above the thoughts that come storming in on them from outside and rise to thoughts that are meaningful for all eternity, they kindle an inner flame that will light their way through the worlds of the soul. When they develop in themselves the higher qualities of equanimity, stillness, and peace in addition to the other qualities we have listed, they feed and maintain the flame. When they become able to remain silent—when instead of bombarding the world with mere words, they live a life of love, so that all of life becomes a religious ritual—the world begins to resound for them. This is what the Pythagoreans called "the music of the spheres." It is not just a symbol; it is a reality. I have been able to give only a few indications of how to reach a path that leads to a narrow gate. It is possible for anyone to reach that narrow gate. It will open to anyone who does not shun the necessary means and effort. And when it opens, it reveals what humanity's great worldviews have always communicated: the one and only eternal truth and the way to life.

2. THE PATH

Berlin

DECEMBER 7, 1905

I have already discussed ideas about the suprasensory world and its relationship with the sensory world in a long series of lectures here. Therefore, it is only natural that the question should repeatedly arise: *Where do these insights into the suprasensory world come from?* This question—in other words, the question of inner development—will occupy us today.

By the phrase "inner human development," I mean the ascent of human beings to the capacities they must acquire for themselves if they wish to have suprasensory insights of their own. However, please do not misunderstand the purpose of this lecture. This lecture will be far from specifying any rules or laws having to do with general human morality or with dictates belonging the general religion of our age. I must stress this because in our day of universal leveling—where no difference is allowed to make a difference between one human being and another—the misunderstanding often arises whenever esotericism is being discussed, that some sort of general demands or fundamental moral laws, valid across the board for all without variation, are being established. This is not the case. This point requires particular clarification in our age of standardization, when differences between human beings are not at all acknowledged.

Neither should today's lecture be mistaken for a lecture concerning the general fundamentals of the theosophical movement. Occultism, or esotericism, is not the same as Theosophy. The Theosophical Society is not alone in practicing esotericism, and certainly to do so is not its only task. A person could well join the Theosophical Society and avoid esotericism altogether.

In the Theosophical Society, one of the things that we cultivate, in addition to the pursuit of a universal ethics, is occultism, or esotericism, which from this point of view has to do with laws of existence that are hidden from the usual sense observation in everyday human experience. Such laws, however, are by no means unrelated to everyday experience. *Occult* means "hidden," or "mysterious." Therefore it must be stressed over and over again that this is a path with certain truly necessary preconditions. Higher mathematics seems incomprehensible to the simple peasant who never encountered it before. In the same way, esotericism seems incomprehensible to many people today. Esotericism, however, ceases to be "occult" [or "hidden"] once it has been mastered. By saying this, I have strictly defined the boundaries of today's lecture.

Therefore no one can object—this must be stressed in the light of many people's experience over the millennia—that the demands of esotericism cannot be fulfilled, that they contradict the general culture. Remember: *no one is required to fulfil these demands.* Those who come to me wanting to hear the truths available through esotericism and nevertheless refuse to walk the path are like schoolchildren who want to electrify a glass rod and refuse to rub it. But, without friction, the rod will not be charged with electricity. This is similar to the objection raised against the practice of esotericism.

No one tells you to become an esotericist. People come to esotericism of their own volition. Those who say we do not need esotericism do not need to bother themselves with it. At this time, esotericism does not appeal to humanity in general. In fact, it is extremely difficult in our culture to submit to the requirements of a life that can open to the spiritual world.

Two preconditions for esotericism are totally lacking in our culture. The first condition is isolation, what esoteric science calls "higher human solitude." The second is the overcoming of what has become the dominant inner soul characteristic of our time— largely unconscious human *egoism*.

The absence of these two preconditions renders the path of inner development simply unattainable. Isolation, or spiritual solitude, is very difficult to achieve because life tends to distract us and disperse our attention—in other words, it demands our external, sensory involvement. In no previous culture have people lived so outwardly as in our own. I beg you, however, not to take what I am saying as a criticism, but simply as an objective characterization.

Of course, whoever speaks as I do knows that this situation cannot be different, and that the greatest advantages and greatest achievements of our time depend upon these characteristics. But this is why our time is so barren of suprasensory insight and why our culture is so devoid of every suprasensory influence. In other cultures—and there are such—human beings are able to cultivate the inner life more than we do and to withdraw from the influences of external life. Such cultures offer a soil where inner life in the higher sense can thrive. In the Eastern cultures, for instance, there is what is called *yoga*. Those who live according to the rules of this teaching are called yogis. A yogi is one who strives for higher spiritual knowledge, but only after seeking a master of the suprasensory. No one in those cultures will seek without the guidance of a master or guru. Once a guru has been found, the yogi must spend much of the day, whether or not with regularity, living wholly within the soul. All the forces that the yogi needs to develop already lie safe within the soul. They exist there as truly as electricity exists in the glass rod before it is produced by friction.

To invoke soul forces in the manner of the yogis, we must use methods of spiritual science that are the results of observations made over millennia. This is very difficult in our time, which (as I said) demands a certain splintering of each individual struggling for existence. A person today cannot achieve complete equanimity—not even the *concept* of composure that the yogis had. There is no consciousness of the deep solitude that yogis must seek. The yogi must repeat the same practice rhythmically with immense regularity, if only for a brief time each day, in total separation from all usual concerns. All the life that usually surrounds one must cease to exist, and one's senses must become unreceptive to all impressions of the world. One must be able to make oneself deaf and dumb to one's surroundings for the prescribed time. The yogi must be able to concentrate to such a degree—and must acquire practice in this concentration—that a cannon could be fired next to him or her without disturbing the attention to the inner life. At the same time, the yogi must also become free of all memory impressions, particularly those of everyday life.

Just think how difficult it is to bring about such conditions in our culture. We don't even have the concept of solitude. Spiritual solitude of this kind must be achieved in such a way that the harmony—the complete equilibrium—with the surrounding world is never lost. But this harmony is very easy to lose while one is deeply absorbed in one's inner life. To go more and more deeply inward requires the capacity to harmonize all the more clearly with the outer world.

No hint of estrangement, of distancing from external practical life, may arise in us lest we stray from the right course. Otherwise, it might be impossible to distinguish our higher life from insanity. Truly, it is a kind of insanity when inner life loses its proper relationship to outer life. Just imagine, for instance, that you know all about our conditions on Earth and that you have all the experience and wisdom that may be gathered here. One day, you fall asleep in the evening; and in the morning you wake up on—not on Earth but on Mars. The conditions on Mars, of course, are quite different from those on Earth; and the knowledge you have gathered on Earth is now useless to you. There is no longer harmony between life within and external life. You would probably find yourself in a Martian insane asylum within an hour! A similar situation could easily arise if the development of one's internal life is cut off from the external world. One must take strict care that this does not happen. These are great difficulties in our culture.

The other obstacle is egoism in relation to inner soul qualities. Present humanity usually takes no account of this. This egoism is closely connected with the spiritual development of humanity. An important prerequisite for spiritual development is *not to seek it out of egoism*. Whoever seeks out of egoism cannot get very far. Human beings in our time are egoistic right into their innermost soul. Again and again the objection is heard, "What is the use of esoteric teachings if I cannot experience them myself?" Those who begin with this presumption and cannot change it have little chance of attaining higher development. For one aspect of higher development is the most intimate awareness of human community, so that it is immaterial whether it is I or another who has the experience.

Given this, I must meet whoever has a higher development than I with unlimited love and trust. First, I must push through to this consciousness of infinite trust toward my fellow human beings when they say that they have had experiences. Such trust is a precondition for working together. Wherever esoteric capacities are strongly brought into play, there exists unlimited trust, for one becomes aware that each human being is a personality in whom a higher individuality lives. Therefore, the first basis for me is trust and faith, because we do not seek the higher self only in ourselves but also in our fellow human beings. Everyone living around us exists in undivided unity in the inner kernel of our being.

It is my lower self that separates me from other humans. But as far as my higher self is concerned—and that alone can ascend to the spiritual world—I am no longer separated from my fellow human beings; I am united with my brothers and sisters. The one speaking to me out of higher truths is actually my own self. I must get away completely from the notion of difference between the other and myself. I must completely overcome the feeling that the other has an advantage over me. Try to live your way into this feeling until it penetrates the most intimate fiber of your soul and causes every vestige of egoism to disappear. Do this so that the one further along the path than you truly stands before you like your own self. If you have done so, then you have attained one of the prerequisites for awakening higher spiritual life.

In situations where one receives guidance for the esoteric life, sometimes quite erroneously and confusedly, one may often hear that the higher self lives in the human being, that one need only allow the inner being to speak and the highest truth will thereby become manifest. Nothing is more correct and, at the same time, less productive than this assertion. Just try to let your inner self speak, and you will see that, as a rule, no matter how much you fancy that your higher self is making an appearance, it is the lower self that speaks. The higher self is, for the time being, not to be found within us. We must seek it outside ourselves. We can learn a good deal from the person who is further along than we are, since there the higher self is visible. One's higher self can gain nothing from one's own egoistic I. Where the one now stands who is further along than I am, I too will stand sometime in the future. I am truly constituted to carry within me the seed for what the other already is. The paths to Olympus, however, must first be illuminated before one can follow them.

A feeling that may seem unbelievable is the fundamental condition for all spiritual development. This feeling is mentioned in all the religions, and every practical and experienced esotericist and occultist can confirm it. Christianity describes it with a well-known saying, which an esotericist must penetrate to the very essence: "*Except ye become … as little children, ye shall not enter the kingdom of heaven*" (Matt. 18:3). Only a person who has learned to revere in the highest sense can understand this sentence. Suppose that in your childhood you heard about a revered person, an individual whom you held in the highest regard, and now you are offered the opportunity to meet this person. You are filled with a sense of awe as the moment approaches when you will see this person for the first time. There, standing on the threshold of the place where this personality sits, you might feel hesitant to touch the door handle and open it. To look up to a personality worthy of reverence in this way is to begin to grasp the feeling that is meant in Christianity when it is said that "one should become like little children in order to enter the kingdom of heaven." It does not really matter whether or not the object of the reverence is truly worthy of it or not. What matters is the capacity to look up to something with a reverence that comes from the innermost heart. This is the meaning of reverence: to be drawn up to what one reveres.

This feeling of reverence is the force—the magnetic power— that raises us to higher spheres of suprasensory life. This is the law of the spiritual world that all who seek the higher life must inscribe into their soul with golden letters. Inner development must start from this basic mood of the soul. Without this feeling of reverence, nothing can be achieved.

In addition to reverence, a person who seeks to develop inwardly must understand clearly that he or she is undertaking something of immense human importance. For what one seeks is nothing less than a new birth: this must be understood literally. The higher human soul must be *born*. Just as we were born with our first birth from the deep inner foundations of existence and then emerged into the light of the Sun, so too, if we seek inner development, we must now step forth from the physical light of the Sun into a higher spiritual light. Something is to be born in us that rests as deeply within us as the unborn child rests in the mother.

Whoever does not know the full significance of this fact does not understand what spiritual development means. The higher soul, resting at first deep within human nature and interwoven with it, is to be brought forth. In the human being who stands before us in everyday life, higher and lower natures are intermingled—which is fortunate for everyday life.

Were it not that there lives alongside our lower nature a higher one that exerts a balancing influence, many of us would, if we followed our lower nature, exhibit evil, negative qualities. This intermingling of lower and higher natures may be compared to mixing a yellow with a blue liquid in a glass. The result is a green liquid in which blue and yellow can no longer be distinguished. Lower and higher human natures are mixed in the same way, and cannot be distinguished from each other. However, just as you can extract the blue liquid from the green by a chemical process, so that only the yellow remains and the unified green is separated into a complete duality, so too the lower and higher human natures separate in spiritual development. One draws one's lower nature out of the body like a sword from the scabbard that then remains alone. The lower nature emerges, appearing almost gruesome. When it was still mixed with the higher nature, nothing of it was noticeable. But once separated, all evil, negative qualities come into view.

People who previously appeared benevolent often become argumentative and jealous. This characteristic existed earlier in the person's lower nature, but was guided by the higher. One can observe this in many who have been guided along an abnormal path. Introduced into the spiritual world, a person may easily become a liar—the capacity to distinguish between true and false is especially easily lost. It is therefore an essential part of esoteric training that alongside that training a most serious training of personal character take place. What history tells us of the saints and their temptations is not legend but the literal truth.

No matter which path is taken, those who try to develop toward the higher world are easily prone to such temptations unless they can develop inner strength and strength of character—and the highest sense of morality—and thus be able to subdue all that they encounter. Not only do lust and passions grow—that is not so much the problem—but opportunities also increase to indulge them. This seems astounding. As if miraculously, those ascending into the higher worlds find previously hidden opportunities for evil lurking around them. In every aspect of life a demon lies in wait, ready to lead them astray. Now they see what they had not before. The division within their own being charms such opportunities from the hidden areas of life. Therefore, a very particular shaping of character is an indispensable foundation for so-called "white magic." This is the school of spiritual development that leads to the higher worlds in a good, true, and genuine way. Every practical esotericist will tell you that no one should dare to step through the "narrow gate"—as the entrance to spiritual development is called—without practicing these qualities over and over. They are the necessary preparation for spiritual life.

First, we must develop the ability to distinguish what is unimportant from what is important in every situation in our lives—that is, we must learn to distinguish what is perishable from what is imperishable. This requirement is easy to state but difficult to accomplish. As Goethe says, "It is easy, but what is easy is hard." For instance, take a plant or an object. You will learn to understand that everything has an important and an unimportant side, and that we are usually interested in what is unimportant—the relationship of the thing to ourselves, or some other subordinate aspect. Whoever wishes to become an esotericist must gradually develop the habit of seeing and seeking in each thing its *essence*. For instance, when we see a clock we must be interested in its laws. We must be able to disassemble it into its smallest parts and to develop a feeling for the laws of the clock. A mineralogist will arrive at considerable knowledge about a quartz crystal simply by looking at it. But the esotericist must be able to take the stone in his or her hand and to feel in a living way something akin to the following: "In a certain sense you, the crystal, are beneath humanity, but in a certain sense you are far above humanity. You are below humanity, because you cannot form a conceptual picture of the human being, and because you do not feel. You cannot explain or think. You do not live, but nevertheless you have an advantage over us. You are pure within yourself, have no desire, no wishes, no lust. Every human, every living being has wishes, desires, lusts. You do not have them. You are complete and without wishes, satisfied with what has come to you, an example for us, with which we shall have to unite our other qualities."

The esotericist who can feel this in all its depth has grasped what the stone can tell him or her. Indeed, in this way one can draw something full of meaning out of everything. Once this has become habitual, when we separate the important from the unimportant, then we have acquired another feeling essential to the esotericist. We must connect our own life with what is important. Here people today err particularly easily. They believe that their place in life is not proper for them. How often people are inclined to say: "My lot has put me in the wrong place." For example, "I am a postal clerk. But if I were placed differently, I could give people high ideas, great teaching," and so on. The mistake that such people make is that they do not go into the significant aspect of their occupation. If, because I can talk to people here, you see in me something of importance, then you do not see the importance of your own life and work. If the mail carriers did not carry the mail, the whole postal traffic would stop, and much work already achieved by others would be in vain. Consequently, everyone in their proper place is exceedingly important for the whole. None is higher than any other. Christ tried to demonstrate this most beautifully in St. John's Gospel: *"The servant is not greater than his lord; neither is he that is sent greater than he that sent him"* (13:16). These words were spoken after the Master washed the feet of the apostles. What he meant was this: "What would I be without my apostles? They must be there so that I can be there in the world, and I must pay tribute to them by lowering myself before them and washing their feet." *This is one of the most significant allusions to the feeling that the esotericist must have for what is important.* What is important in the inward sense must not be confused with what seems outwardly important. This must be strictly observed.

In addition to this, we must develop a further series of qualities. To begin with, we must become masters over our thoughts, and particularly our train of thought. This is called *control of thoughts.* Just think how thoughts whirl about in our soul, how they flit like will-o'-the-wisps. Here one impression arises, there another, and each changes our thoughts. It is not true that we govern our thoughts. Our thoughts govern us totally. We must come to the point that at a given time in the day we can become so absorbed in a thought that no other thought can enter and disturb our soul. In this way we ourselves hold the reins of thought-life for a time.

The second quality is to find a similar relationship to our actions, that is, to exercise *control over our actions.* Here it is necessary to act, at least occasionally, in ways that are not initiated by anything external. Whatever is initiated by our station in life, our profession, or our situation does not lead us more deeply into higher life. Higher life depends on such intimate things as resolving to do something that springs completely from our own initiative—even if it is something absolutely insignificant. All other actions contribute nothing to the higher life.

The third quality to strive for is *equanimity.* People fluctuate back and forth between joy and sorrow. One moment they are beside themselves with joy, the next they are unbearably sad. Thus we allow ourselves to be rocked on the waves of life, on joy or sorrow. We must reach equanimity and steadiness. Neither the greatest sorrow nor the greatest joy must unsettle our composure. We must become steadfast and even-tempered.

The fourth soul quality is to *understand every being.* Nothing expresses more beautifully what it means to understand every being than the legend handed down to us, not by the Gospel, but by a Persian story. Jesus was walking across a field with his disciples. As they went, they encountered the decaying corpse of a dog. The animal looked horrible. Jesus stopped and cast an admiring look upon it, saying, "What beautiful teeth that animal has!" Within the ugly, Jesus found the one beautiful aspect. Strive at all times to approach what is wonderful in every object of outer reality. You will see that everything contains an aspect that can be affirmed. Do as Christ did when he admired the beautiful teeth of the dead dog. Practicing this will lead you to the great ability to tolerate everything, and to an understanding of everything and of every being.

The fifth quality is *complete openness* toward everything new that meets us. Most people judge the new things they meet by the old that they already know. If anyone comes to tell them something new, they immediately respond with an opposing opinion. But we must not confront a new communication immediately with our own opinion. We must rather be on the alert for possibilities of learning something new. And learn we can, even from a small child. Even if one were the wisest person, one must be willing to hold back one's own judgment and listen to others. We must develop this ability to listen, for it will enable us to meet matters with the greatest possible openness. In esotericism, this is called "faith." It is the power not to weaken through opposition the impression made by the new.

The sixth quality is something we all receive once we have developed the first five. This is *inner harmony.* Those who have the other qualities are also inwardly harmonious. Furthermore, it is necessary for those seeking spiritual development to develop their *feeling for freedom* to the highest degree. The feeling for freedom enables us to seek within ourselves the center of our being, to stand on our own two feet, so that we will not have to ask everyone what we should do and so can stand upright and act freely. This also is a quality that one needs to acquire.

Once we have developed these inner qualities, then we stand above all the dangers that can arise from the division in human nature. The qualities of our lower nature can no longer affect us—we can no longer stray from the path. Therefore, these qualities must be formed with the greatest precision. Then we enter the esoteric life—the expression of which requires a certain "rhythmization" in life.

The phrase *carrying rhythm into life* expresses the unfolding of this faculty. Observe nature, and you will find a certain rhythm.

You will expect the violet to bloom every year at the same time in spring, and the crops in the field and the grapes on the vine to ripen at the same time each year. In nature, this rhythmical sequence of phenomena exists everywhere. There is rhythm, repetition in regular sequence, everywhere. However, as you ascend from the plant toward more highly developed beings, you will find the rhythmic sequence decreasing. Nevertheless, even in the higher stages of animal development, one can see how all functions are rhythmically ordered. Animals acquire certain functions and capabilities at a given time each year. And yet, the higher a being evolves, the more life is given over into the hands of the being itself, and the more these rhythms cease. We see this in the various bodies. (You know that the physical body is only one member of the human being. There are also the etheric body, the astral body, and, finally, the higher members that form the basis for the others.)

Now, the physical body is subject to the same rhythm that governs outer nature. Just as plant and animal life, in its external form, takes its course rhythmically, so does the life of the physical body. The heart beats rhythmically, the lungs breathe rhythmically, and so forth. All this proceeds so rhythmically because it is set in order by higher powers, by the wisdom of the world, by what the Scriptures call the *Holy Spirit*. The higher bodies, particularly the astral body, have been, as it were, abandoned by these higher spiritual forces. They have lost their rhythm. Can you deny that your activity relating to wishes, desires, and passions is irregular, that it can in no way compare with the regularity ruling the physical body? Whoever learns to know the rhythm inherent in physical nature increasingly finds in it the image of spirituality. If you consider the heart, this wonderful organ with the regular beat and innate wisdom, and you compare it with the desires and passions of the astral body that unleash all sorts of actions against the heart, you will recognize how its regular course is influenced detrimentally by passion. *The functions of the astral body must become as rhythmical as those of the physical body.*

I want to mention something here that will seem outlandish to most people. This is the matter of fasting. Consciousness of the meaning of fasting has been completely lost. Fasting is enormously significant, however, for rhythmizing our astral body. What does it mean to fast? It means to restrain the desire to eat, to block the astral body in relation to this desire. One who fasts blocks the astral body and develops no desire to eat. This is like blocking a force in a machine. The astral body becomes inactive then, and the whole rhythm of the physical body with its innate wisdom works upward into the astral body to give it rhythm. Like the imprint of a seal, the harmony of the physical body impresses itself upon the astral body. It would transfer much more permanently if the astral body were not continuously being made irregular by desires, passions, and wishes, including spiritual desires and wishes.

It is more necessary today than it was in earlier times for human beings to bring rhythm into all spheres of higher life. Just as rhythm is implanted in the physical body by God, so we must make our own astral bodies rhythmical. We must order our day for ourselves. We must arrange the rhythm of our day for the astral body as the spirit of nature arranges it for the lower realms. In the morning, at a definite time, one must undertake one spiritual action; a different one must be undertaken at another time, again to be adhered to regularly, and yet another in the evening. These spiritual exercises must not be chosen arbitrarily, but must be suitable for the development of the higher life. This is one method for taking life in hand and for keeping it in hand. So set a time for yourself in the morning when you can *concentrate*. Stick to this time. Establish a kind of calm so that the esoteric master in you may awaken. You must *meditate* on a great thought content that has nothing to do with the outer world. Let this thought content come to life completely within you. A short time will suffice for this—perhaps a quarter of an hour. Even five minutes are enough if more time is not available. *It is worthless to do these exercises irregularly.* You must do them regularly so that the activity of the astral body becomes regular as a clock. Only then do they have value. If you do these exercises regularly, the astral body will appear completely different. Sit down in the morning and do these exercises, and the forces I have described will develop. But, as I said, you must do this *regularly*, for the astral body expects that the same process will take place at the same time each day, and it falls into disorder if this does not happen. At least, the intent toward order must exist. If you rhythmize your life in this way, you will see success before too long—in other words, the spiritual life hidden from you for the time being will manifest to a certain degree.

As a rule, human life alternates among four states. The first state is *perception* of the outer world. You look around with your senses and perceive the outer world. The second is what we may call *imagination* or the life of mental *images* that is related to, or even part of, dream life. Here we are not rooted in our surroundings, but rather separated from them. In this state we have, for the most part, no realities before us, but mostly recollections, reminiscences. The third state is *dreamless sleep*, in which we have no self-awareness at all. Finally, in the fourth state, we live in *memory*. This is different from perception. It is already something remote, spiritual. If we had no memory in this sense, we could not undertake spiritual development.

Inner life begins to develop by means of inner contemplation and meditation. If we practice this, then sooner or later we begin to notice that we no longer dream in a chaotic manner. In fact, we begin to dream in the most meaningful way. Remarkable things begin to reveal themselves in our dreams—things that we gradually begin to recognize as manifestations of spiritual beings. Naturally, the trivial objection might easily be raised that this is nothing but a dream and therefore "So what?" However, should someone discover, for instance, the dirigible balloon in a dream and then proceed to build it, surely the dream would simply have shown the truth. Thus, an idea can be grasped in an unusual way and the truthfulness of it can then be judged by the fact that it can be realized. We must become convinced of its inner truth from outside.

The next step in spiritual life is to comprehend truth by means of our own qualities. At the same time, we must begin to guide our dreams consciously. When we begin to guide our dreams in a regular manner, then we are at the stage where truth becomes transparent for us. Here, again, there are a number of stages.

The first stage is called *material* cognition. For this, the object must lie before us. The next stage is *imaginative* cognition. It is developed through meditation—through shaping life rhythmically. Achieving this is laborious. But once it is achieved, the time arrives when there is no longer a difference between ordinary perception and perception in the suprasensory. When we are among the things of our ordinary lives—that is, when we are in the sense world—and we then change our spiritual state, then we continuously experience the spiritual, suprasensory world. But this will happen only if we have trained ourselves sufficiently. It happens once we are able to become deaf and dumb to the sense world to remember nothing of the everyday world, and at the same time still retain a spiritual life within us. Then our dream life begins to assume a conscious form. If we are then able to pour some of this into our everyday life, the next capacity arises. This renders the soul-qualities of the beings around us perceptible, and we see not only the outer aspect of things but also the inner, hidden essential kernel of plants, animals, and human beings. I know that many people will say that these are actually different things. And it is true, they are different from what a person sees who does not have these senses.

The third stage occurs when our consciousness—which we have been able to completely empty—begins to be enlivened by the entry of *continuous consciousness*. This continuity appears on its own. Then we are no longer unconscious during sleep. During the time when we used to sleep, we now experience the spiritual world.

Generally speaking, what is sleep? The physical body lies in bed, and the astral body lives in the suprasensory world. You go for a walk in this suprasensory world. As a rule, a person with the type of disposition that is typical today cannot withdraw very far from the body. However, when you practice the rules given by spiritual science, organs are developed in the astral body as it wanders during sleep. These allow one to become conscious during sleep. Just as the physical body has organs, the astral body can develop them too. The physical body would be blind and deaf if it had no eyes or ears, and the astral body wandering at night is blind and deaf for the same reason, because it does not yet have eyes and ears.

These organs are developed through meditation. This provides the means for training these organs. Meditation must then be practiced regularly. It is practiced in such a way that the physical body is its mother and the human spirit is its father. The physical human body, as we see it before us, is in each one of its parts a mystery. Indeed, every aspect of the physical body is related in a definite but mysterious way to a part of the astral body. These are matters with which the esotericist is familiar. For example, the point in the physical body lying between the eyebrows belongs to a certain organ in the astral organism. When the esotericist indicates how one must direct thoughts, feelings, and sensations to this point between the eyebrows, then—by connecting something formed in the physical body with the corresponding part of the astral body—the result will be a certain sensation in the astral body. But this must be practiced regularly, and one must know how to do it. In this way, the astral body begins to form its members. From a lump, it grows to be a system in which organs are formed. I have described the astral sense organs in the periodical *Lucifer-Gnosis.*[1] They are also called lotus flowers. We can cultivate these lotus flowers by means of special word sequences. Once this

---

1. The term *Lucifer* is used here in its literal meaning, "bearer of light." Steiner edited *Luzifer: The Periodical for the Life of the Soul, Spiritual Culture, and Theosophy* published from June, 1903 until January 1904, when it became *Lucifer-Gnosis*; altogether, there were 34 issues, collected in *Lucifer-Gnosis, 1903–1908* (Dornach, 1960), not translated.

has occurred, we can perceive the spiritual world. This is the same world one enters when one passes through the gate of death. In other words, Hamlet was wrong when he spoke of "The undiscover'd country from whose bourn no traveller returns."

So it is possible to go, or rather to slip, from the sense world into the suprasensory world and to live there as well as here. That does not mean life in cloud-cuckoo-land, but life in a realm that clarifies and explains life in our realm. Just as the typical person who has not studied electricity would not understand all the wonderful mechanisms in a factory powered by electricity, so the average person does not understand what happens in the spiritual world. Visitors to a factory will not understand the power involved until they know the laws of electricity. Similarly, we cannot understand the realm of the spirit until we know the laws of spirit. There is nothing in our world that is not dependent on the spiritual world at every moment. Everything surrounding us is the external expression of the spiritual world. There is no materiality. Everything material is condensed spirit. For the person looking into the spiritual world, the whole material, sensory perceptible world—the world in general—becomes spiritualized. As ice melts into water through the effect of the Sun, so everything sensory perceptible melts into something spiritual within the soul that looks into the spiritual world. Thus, the foundation of the world gradually manifests to the spiritual eye and ear.

The life that we learn to know in this way is actually the spiritual life we have borne within us all along. We know nothing of it, however, because—until we have developed our organs for the higher worlds—*we do not know ourselves*. Imagine possessing the qualities you now have, without having sensory organs. You would know nothing of the world around you. You would not understand the physical body, yet you would belong to the physical world. Likewise, the human soul belongs to the spiritual world, but does not know it because the soul does not hear or see it. As our body is drawn out of the forces and materials of the physical world, so our soul is drawn out of the forces and materials of the spiritual world.

We do not recognize ourselves within ourselves, but only within our surroundings. We cannot perceive a heart or brain, even using X-rays, without using our sense organs to see it (eyes are needed to see the heart), and we really cannot see or hear our own soul without perceiving it with spiritual organs in the surrounding world. You can know yourself only through your surroundings.

In truth, there is no inner knowledge, no self-contemplation; there is only one knowledge, one revelation of the life around us, given to us through the organs of both the physical and the spiritual bodies. We belong to the worlds around us—to the physical, soul, and spiritual worlds. If we have physical organs, we can learn from the physical world, if we have spiritual and soul organs, we can learn from the spiritual world and from all souls. There is no cognition other than cognition of the world.

It is vain and empty idleness for someone to "brood" inwardly, believing that it is possible to progress simply by looking within. We will find the God in ourselves if we awaken the divine organs within us and find our higher divine self in our surroundings, just as we find our lower self only through the use of our eyes and ears. We perceive ourselves clearly as physical beings by means of intercourse with the sensory world, and we perceive ourselves clearly in relation to the spiritual world by developing spiritual senses. Inner development means opening ourselves to the divine life around us.

You will now understand why it is essential that anyone who ascends to the higher world undergoes, to begin with, an immense strengthening of character. Human beings can experience the characteristics of the sense world on their own, because their senses are already opened. This is possible because a benevolent divine spirit, who has seen and heard in the physical world, stood by humankind in the most ancient times, before human beings could see and hear, and opened their eyes and ears. It is from such beings that we must learn now to see spiritually: from beings who are already able to do what we still must learn to do. We must have a guru who can tell us how we should develop our organs, one who will tell us what he or she has done to develop those organs. Whoever wishes to guide others in this way must have acquired one fundamental quality—*unconditional truthfulness.* This same quality is also a chief requirement for the student. No one may train to become an esotericist unless this fundamental quality of unconditional truthfulness has been previously cultivated.

One can test whatever is said of sensory experience. But when I tell you something about the spiritual world, you must *trust,* because you are not advanced enough to confirm that information yourselves. One who wishes to be a guru must become so truthful that it is impossible to take statements lightly that concern the spirit world or spiritual life. The sensory world corrects our errors immediately by its own nature; in the spiritual world, we must have these guidelines within ourselves. We must be strictly trained, so that we are not forced to use the outer world for controls but only our inner self. We are only able to gain this control by acquiring *in this world* the strictest truthfulness. Therefore, when the Theosophical Society began to present some of the basic teachings of esotericism to the world, it had to adopt the principle: *there is no law higher than truth.*

Very few understand this principle. Most are satisfied with saying they are convinced of a truth, and if it proves wrong, they simply say they were mistaken. Esotericists cannot rely on subjective honesty. If they do, they are on the wrong track. They must always be in harmony with the facts of the external world, and any experience that contradicts these facts must be seen as an error or a mistake. For the esotericist, the question of who is at fault for an error ceases to be important. Esotericists must be in absolute harmony with the facts in life. They must begin to feel responsible in the strictest sense for every assertion. If they wish to be spiritual guides, they must have unconditional certainty, both for themselves and for others. Therefore they must train themselves in this.

We will have to speak about these matters again in order to add the higher concepts, but today I needed to indicate a series of qualities and methods. It may seem to you that these things are too intimate to discuss with others, that each soul must come to grips with them on its own terms. Many may also feel that they are ill-suited for reaching the great goal we should reach—that is, entering the spiritual world. But this entrance will certainly be reached by all those who tread the path I have characterized.

When? One of the most outstanding participants in the theosophical movement, Subba Rao, who died some time ago, has spoken fittingly of this.[2] Replying to the question of how long it would take, he said, "Seven years, perhaps also seven times seven years, perhaps even seven incarnations, perhaps only seven hours." It all depends on what we bring into life. We may meet a person who seems very stupid, but has brought into life a concealed *higher* life that merely needs only to be revealed. Most people these days are much farther along than it seems, and more would know of this if the materialism that conditions our time did not force them back into the inner life of the soul. Most people today have previously advanced much farther. Many factors will determine whether what is within them will emerge. But it is possible to give some help. Imagine that, there before you, stands a person who was highly developed in an earlier incarnation, but whose brain is now undeveloped. Such a brain may conceal great spiritual faculties. Consequently, if that person is taught the usual, ordinary abilities, inner spirituality may also develop.

Another important factor is a person's environment. In a very significant way, human beings are mirror images of their surroundings. Imagine one who is a highly developed individual, but lives in surroundings that awaken and develop certain prejudices with such a strong effect that the higher talents cannot unfold. Unless such a person finds someone who can draw out these abilities, they will remain hidden.

---

2. Subba Rao (1856–1890), a lawyer in Madras, India, was an esotericist and a friend of H. P. Blavatsky. His *Esoteric Writings* was published posthumously.

I have been able to give only a few indications to you about this matter. I especially wanted to awaken in you this one understanding, that the higher life is not schooled in a tumultuous way but rather quite intimately, in the deepest soul, and that the great day when the soul awakens and enters into the higher life actually arrives like the thief in the night. The development toward the higher life leads us into a new world, and when we have entered this new world, then we see the other side of existence, so to speak. Then we see that what has previously been hidden for us reveals itself. It may occur to you that not everyone might be able to do this; perhaps only a few can do it. But that must not prevent you from at least beginning on the way that is open to all—that is, hearing about higher worlds. Human beings are called to live in community. Whoever is cut off cannot arrive at a spiritual life. Some cut themselves off in a higher sense by saying, "I don't believe this, it does not relate to me; it might be valid for the afterlife." This kind of thinking has no value for the esotericist. It is fundamental for esotericists to consider other human beings as true manifestations of their own higher self, because then they realize that they must find the other in themselves.

There is a delicate distinction between these two sentences: "To find the others in oneself," and "To find oneself in the others." In the higher sense, it means, "You are that" [*tat tsvam asi*].

Above all, in the highest sense, it means to recognize oneself in the world and to understand that saying of Novalis from *The Disciples at Sais* that I quoted some weeks ago in a different context: "One was successful. He lifted the veil of the goddess at Sais. But what did he see? Miracle of miracles! He saw himself." To find oneself—not in egoistic inwardness, but selflessly in the outer world—that is true self-knowledge.

3. First Steps

Berlin

Today I would like to speak to you again about inner development. Those of you who have attended these lectures frequently will recall various earlier presentations on this subject, so I will merely touch upon matters that have already been discussed and then proceed to take them further.

Since we have heard repeatedly about the facts and phenomena of higher worlds, the obvious question is, how do we acquire direct, personal knowledge of them? The path to such knowledge is not so easy that it can be described even superficially in an hour or two. Occasionally, however, it is necessary to suggest how we should imagine the development of such knowledge. You all know that we are talking not only about the ordinary physical world but also about the world of soul and the world of spirit, which we have learned to call the astral world and the *devachan*.[1] We human beings dwell in all of these worlds, belonging to all three rather than just one. In reality, we belong to many more worlds as well, but those still higher worlds are so far beyond the present scope of human knowledge that it would be difficult to talk about them.

The question we must ask ourselves now is, how do we make our way up into the astral and spiritual worlds? Although we live in these two worlds, we know nothing about them initially. Once we are no longer clothed in sensory perceptible bodies, we will dwell in the astral and spiritual worlds, and the entire sensory realm that now surrounds us will no longer mean anything to us. Those other worlds, however, which can be reached through higher knowledge, will increase in significance. The question is often asked, What is the point of knowing about any world other than the one in which we live? Why worry about higher worlds as long as we are good to our fellow human beings? We soon realize that such rationalizations are meaningless.

The forces, facts, and beings we encounter in higher worlds are active not only there but in our physical world as well. Objects and events in the physical world are not self-creating; they were brought about by forces of the spiritual world. Self-knowledge acquired only through our senses is also superficial, because our senses reveal only the aspect of ourselves that is played out between birth and death. The birth of each individual brings a large number of abilities and potentials into the world. Considering this whole world of potentials, it is shallow to say that birth or conception is the point in time when an individual begins to exist.

In esotericism, which studies worlds unknown to the senses, it is said that ordinary human beings are denied the ability to distinguish the most important facts. They fail to observe closely enough how helpless human beings are when born into this world and how they then gradually learn to use certain organs, which are initially present only in the form of potentials, as organs of the spiritual life. We encounter some people who know very little about how to use their organs of the spirit, whereas others have

---

1. *Devachan* (Sanskrit) = literally "dwelling of the gods," an intermediate state between two earthly lives. The human I-being (the unified *Atma, Buddhi,* and *Manas*) enters this condition after separating from the subjective self and the lower human aspects after death on Earth.

mastered not only their limbs but also the tools of the brain to an exceptional extent. Materialistic thinkers in particular would be forced to say that, although they believe in the importance of human organs, they wonder how these organs can adapt to the feelings and sensations of very different individuals.

Everyone admits that a hammer, which we use in rational ways and for constructive purposes, must have come about as a result of rational human thought and work. Everyone believes this to be true of a hammer, but materialistic thinkers do not believe that this is true of a body or a living being. No one who studies the wonderful structure of the human brain or heart can possibly believe that these organs came about through blind approximation or events devoid of spirit. These organs, however, are constituted differently in each human being and differently in humans than they are in animals. Animals are all copies of a general plan; their particular differences are less important. The word *individuality* makes the difference between humans and animals suddenly clear to us. Because each human being is an individuality, each human individual must be considered to a much greater extent. Each human being prepares his or her body individually, because this body must be adapted to the individual's specific potentials.

Human beings enter this existence through birth after having existed on a spiritual level where they prepared their organs for their own use—although not to the ultimate extent, since human beings are also animal beings. The more highly individuals evolve, however, the more they themselves determine the structure of their own organs. Although we might think that a human being at the lowest stage of development must have existed only since birth, no rational thinker can assume that a thinking being did not exist prior to birth. Anyone can use a hammer, but no one can use the brains of others on their behalf. This means that it is impossible to understand human beings without assuming that they transcend birth and death. We understand human beings only when we have acknowledged the forces that did the preliminary work on the organs of human thinking.

An individual's ascent into the astral and spiritual worlds is associated with certain difficulties, dangers, and necessary renunciations. We are less accustomed to these other worlds than we are to the world of the senses. Above all, we must realize that many causes remain concealed from us in the sensory world and become clear only in the higher worlds; this realization surprises and alarms us. In addition, the exercises that help us in this ascent are strenuous in some ways. Because of the dangers, some people claim that it is possible to achieve the highest knowledge of the divine forces of the cosmos without knowing anything about the spiritual and astral forces concealed behind the sensory world. Nowadays people even say that it is possible to rise to knowledge of the divine without first really passing through the worlds that separate us from the Most High.

Such talk is possible only for those who have no real idea of the higher worlds. One type of higher knowledge that is often called theosophical is nothing more than very ordinary knowledge of the lower human self. No matter how often we call the lower self the god within, we will still find nothing more than our lower self. The higher self is to be found only beyond ourselves, because we have been born out of the outer world. In many spiritual movements people are directed away from the outer world, being advised to seek the higher self only within themselves. This perspective can never lead to true knowledge; it is both unchristian and anti-christian. We discover our higher self only by returning to the world that surrounds us. We seek the godhead in the invisible worlds and in all outer creatures, phenomena, and processes.

Anyone who tells us to deny the outer world because outer matter does not exist is denying the divine world. From a broader perspective, the worst form of knowledge is one that turns away from the outer world. It is immersion in the outer world that leads to higher knowledge. Everything bodily withers when it is raised even slightly above Earth, and everything of a soul nature withers when lifted even slightly out of the spiritual world. Living in the world out of which we are born, and to which we belong as the hand belongs to the body, is a prerequisite to the attitude that truly leads to higher development. Ask your inner self where the meaning of being human lies. It is impossible for this meaning to be enclosed within our skin, just as it is impossible for human beings to turn away from the outer world. We belong to the world's higher self, and we search for our own higher self by searching for the cosmic higher self.

It is not possible to recruit people to the esoteric way. Only those who truly want to set out on this path and who are willing to meet the requirements of higher development may claim to be following the guidelines of esotericism. For this reason, the true esoteric movement in theosophy, which involves methods that have been tested for hundreds of years, should not be confused with what is often superficially called theosophy. Exactly when the goal will be achieved is left to each person's free will, so being an outsider is not a valid excuse.

Higher development, which anyone can achieve, proceeds slowly and gradually. We already dwell, and indeed we always dwell, in the world that we will be able to see only later. None of you are alive only in the sensory world; you are also positively surrounded, here and now, by the forces of soul and spirit and by spiritual events. The worlds of soul and spirit are present for anyone whose soul-spiritual eyes have been opened, and there are methods available for opening those eyes. Only when this has happened does an individual become alive as far as the higher worlds are concerned, because there is a difference between living in these worlds and being able to perceive in them. We are all living *now* in those worlds during the night, but we do not perceive them because we still lack the necessary organs. Higher development requires that the soul acquire its own organs and the ability to perceive with them.

All higher vision awakens first during the night. For human beings who perceive only with the usual senses, the night is dark, but its darkness is illuminated for those who perceive on a soul level. A light exists that can illuminate the world even in the absence of the Sun. This light does not make a table perceptible, but it does reveal soul phenomena. If you have soul organs—that is, if your soul is not blind—the astral light can reveal a person's soul where your eyes previously perceived his or her form. The soul is then illuminated by astral light, just as the body is illuminated by sunlight during the day. All the qualities that are to be developed in us are already present as potentials. Just as the human embryo has the potential to develop eyes and ears, potentials for clairvoyance are present in the soul living within each human being. But just as a human embryo cannot yet see in the physical world, an individual's soul and spirit potentials also need to be developed. With regard to the soul world, we are actually in the embryonic stage. Later, the soul and spirit will see what they do not yet see.

At this point, we must begin to consider what the soul does during sleep. The soul is not inactive during sleep, even if it does not see. The forces of the physical human being are exhausted during the course of the day, but during sleep the human soul works to restore these forces. And because the soul is busy with its own affairs, it has no forces available for developing new organs. The soul's forces must be adequate, however, if something new is to develop, because this new development withdraws forces from the human body. The human spirit gradually built up the physical body, and, so too, the soul gradually builds up the tools the human being needs. The soul works in the same way when the physical body has been exhausted, putting everything in order again during sleep.

If the forces of sleep are used for a different purpose, substitutes must be created for them. Everything that is lost in the battle between forces can be replaced by harmony between forces. People today work constantly; they bow to every will impulse and they feel, will, and think haphazardly in response to every sensation. This struggle exhausts their forces. If people then want to withdraw certain soul forces from the body, they must offer the body certain harmonizing processes as substitutes. Inner development initially prescribes very specific virtues so that the force being withdrawn from the body is replaced by rhythm. These virtues are: control of thoughts, control of actions, positivity, perseverance, equanimity, and trust in one's entire surroundings [see "Six Essential Exercises" in chapter 4].

Today we succumb to every thought that occurs to us, but we ourselves must be the ones to rein in our thoughts. By doing so, we fill ourselves with rhythm. Carrying out actions on our own initiative, making each action we undertake our very own, provides the peace the soul needs. Perseverance: standing fast, allowing joy and sorrow to simply wash over us. Equanimity: allowing neither pleasure nor pain to derail us. In addition, we must acquire the greatest possible positivity. Nothing is more exhausting than seeing the negative aspect of things; it is both disharmonizing and exhausting. A Persian legend—the ultimate example of positivity—tells of how Christ Jesus and his disciples once saw a dead and rotting dog lying in the road. The disciples begged the Master not to bother with the dog; the animal was just too ugly. The Christ, however, looked at the dog and said, "What beautiful teeth the animal has." He was looking for beauty in this ugly situation. An affirmative attitude is always enlivening, while negativity is exhausting and deadening. Not only does addressing the positive aspect of a situation require moral strength, but positivity always has an enlivening effect as well, making the soul's forces independent and strong.

In an age such as ours, nervousness is also very prevalent. Nervousness and criticism go hand in hand. The purpose of the prescribed virtues is to release higher forces and make them available to the individual. Such virtues are intended to make all of our lower life rhythmical and to provide the soul with forces that it can dedicate to higher development. This inner development proceeds very quietly.

I would still like to enumerate a few of the steps of inner development. These steps used to be kept secret by esoteric schools, but for various reasons they can now be communicated. When people have prepared their souls through such practices, any teacher they may find will lead them further. They then pass through various stages of discipleship during which the forces that become available to them must be applied to their higher soul life.

The first step is to realize that one's individual opinion is essentially worthless. More advanced students of the esoteric must thoroughly overcome personal opinion, the tendency to say, "This is what I think" or "That is what I believe." For example, they must not only recognize the foolishness of materialists but must also personally weigh the very good reasons materialists may have for their viewpoint so as to understand how people come to be materialists. Students will find that whenever people say "yes" to anything, thus affirming its positive aspect, they are usually right. Saying "no" marks the beginning of what advanced students must learn to overcome. Such students must be familiar with the contents and foundations of every worldview, both logically and as a result of personal experience. They must be able to slip into the soul of every doubter. Higher forces will not awaken for those who are not familiar with all possible objections. Those who submit to this process, however, can be quite confident that such forces will awaken in their souls.

Second, students of esotericism must overcome every kind of superstition—not only the superstition of primitive fetishists, but also that of more enlightened minds. Everyone is aware of the effects of hypnosis, which our European professors (Wundt, for example) have explained by stating that certain parts of the brain are not well supplied with blood.[2] This statement is no different from primitive superstitions. In this way you would basically be able to refute all materialistic theories that talk only about certain

---

2. Wilhelm Wundt (1832–1920), German physiologist and psychologist, considered the founder of experimental psychology. A student of Johannes Müller, he believed psychology should be based on immediate experience and prescribed a methodology of introspection. He authored many works.

parts of the brain.[3] No matter how great Haeckel may be as a research scientist, it must be clear to everyone that his statements are pure superstition.[4] The esoteric student must overcome superstition in all its forms.

The third step is to recognize that the personal self is an illusion and that it is illusory to persuade ourselves that we can discover the higher life within ourselves. Anyone who has achieved this insight is ready for the second level. We must transcend the illusion of the personal self, but we must recognize its legitimacy in order to free ourselves of it.

The next step is to allow everything to become an allegory: "Everything transient is but an allegory" [*Faust* 2]. Everything must be seen for what it actually is, namely, an allegory of what it brings to expression. An individual flower, even an individual human being, must become an allegory for students of the esoteric, who will then feel how this attitude causes forces to awaken in their souls.

After spending some time learning to see all things as allegories, esoteric students must then learn that the human being is a microcosm, that there is nothing within the human being that does not have its counterpart in the external macrocosm. There is deep meaning in the Germanic myth that tells how the whole world was formed out of the giant Ymir [a Nordic god, father of the giants]. Esoteric students must learn how each organ relates to the world in order to know how to bring their own bodies into the right relationship to the world. As we make our way through the world in everyday life, we are unaware of how our organs

---

3. In other words, the physiological changes in the brain are not necessarily the *cause* of the hypnotic state but are coincident with it.

4. Ernst Heinrich Philipp August Haeckel (1834–1919) studied science and medicine at the Zoological Institute in Jena; he became the director there as well as professor of comparative anatomy. By the age of sixty he had published 42 works, including: *General Morphology* (1866) and *The History of Creation*. One of his most popular books was *The Riddle of the Universe*. Steiner and Haeckel wrote to each other frequently.

relate to it. These relationships need to be learned. Eastern esotericists teach them by having their students assume a particular sitting posture so that they are brought, even outwardly, into the right relationship to the world.

Something else that must be learned can be mentioned only briefly here, namely, the conscious regulation of processes that are otherwise unconscious and regulated naturally. This applies first and foremost to the respiratory system. Those who choose to pursue higher development must adapt their breathing to the great evolutionary processes, inhaling in a specific, prescribed way, holding the breath, and breathing out again. When people learn to bring the order of the spirit into their breathing, they spiritualize the breath of life and take the step from hatha yoga to raja yoga, the yoga of kings.

The highest of these exercises consist of dwelling within oneself in meditation and contemplation. When esoteric students have prepared and practiced and have advanced to the point of rhythmizing their life, they are completely ready to lead an inner life. There are three levels of meditation; they can be incorporated organically into the process of rhythmic breathing. The point of departure is the world of the senses, so that we learn to divert our attention from the outer world and its plethora of external impressions. By taking total control of our attention, we promote the process of higher development. Once we are able to master our attention in this way, we must also learn to immerse ourselves totally in an object, allowing no other thought to claim our attention; only a single thought must be alive in us. Ideally, a teacher should give very specific assignments appropriate to the student's individuality. Esoteric students must reach the point where a cannon could be fired off next to them without causing distraction. At this point they must abandon the object of their contemplation but retain the activity itself. This is what leads to the highest worlds.

Once we have brought it to this point—thinking the object through, then letting it go and dwelling only on the activity—we achieve the condition known in esotericism as *dhyana*.[5] We can let go of this condition immediately; then our inner eye is awakened.

We learn to exercise our powers of thinking by applying them to outer objects. This does not get us very far; we simply come to a world that appears to be a kind of skeleton for the higher world. At this point we must develop a feeling of particular intensity, based on the object of our attention. Once again, we exclude any other thought content. We must be able to have a very specific feeling when we hold a crystal or an octahedron in our hands. This is the feeling we can have when we encounter the lifeless world. We then compare the lifeless stone to a living, blood-filled, sensual being. In contrast, the stone, clear as water, is free of desire. I feel how the stone has allowed its desire to die and has become pure and chaste. I immerse myself in this feeling, which may come from either a crystal, an animal, or a human being, until the world dies away around me; I permit only the feeling to be alive in me. When I then allow the object of my contemplation to fall away and enter the condition of dhyana as before, I notice that the feeling is not merely a feeling, but begins to grow light; the feeling begins to become a figure of light. In this way, something we perceive as a thought form appears, although it might better be called a feeling form.

These are the individual concepts that I wanted to give you today. There have always been teachers who provide guidance and tasks suited to each student's individuality. In the spiritual world, each human being has an individual name. We are much more individual in that world than we are in the physical world, and this individuality must be taken carefully into account whenever higher development is involved. This is why only a teacher can provide what is needed.

---

5. *Dhyana* (Sanskrit) = literally, "contemplation." One of the six perfections, or *paramitas*. A state of abstraction that carries the practitioner far above the region of sensory perception and out of the world of matter. The other perfections are generosity, moral conduct, patience, courage, and wisdom.

Today I have provided you with the first few steps in the process known as "recognizing the self." When we learn to feel the objects around us and see them take on color that then crystallizes into images, we see the world of our feelings displayed around us. We must then be able to confront ourselves objectively. When we are able to do so, we cross the threshold where we perceive ourselves along with everything we are and are not yet. The first guardian of the threshold stands before us, saying "Behold yourself!"[6] We must learn to recognize ourselves, because knowledge of the world is acquired through self-knowledge. No one, however, is permitted to mistake self-knowledge for knowledge of the divine. That is why the words "know yourself" stood at the portal of the Delphic temple. Having gone through self-knowledge, we enter the cosmic holiest of holies, where divine forces hold sway and spiritual knowledge is imparted. It first becomes possible to speak of inner development in the truest sense when our own inner being feels bound up with the inner being of the world. This spiritual knowledge becomes our own when we approach it worthily, rather than frivolously or in a lower manner. We are then given something that permits our humanity to be ever more developed; we become increasingly worthy participants in the process of humanity's evolution. But we should never aspire to higher knowledge for the sake of our individual selves. We should develop and enhance our powers—and acquiring knowledge means enhancing our powers—only in order to serve the entire universe. The ascent to higher knowledge is meant to take place only with this end in mind.

---

6. The expression "Guardian of the Threshold" comes from Bulwer Lytton's *Zanoni* (Garber communications, Blauvelt, NY, 1989). Steiner speaks in various places about the so-called greater and lesser guardians; see "The Threshold of the Spiritual World" in *A Way of Self-Knowledge* and *How to Know Higher Worlds*.

4. WAYS TO INNER DEVELOPMENT

Stuttgart

SEPTEMBER 2 – 5, 1906

Six Essential Exercises

There is a universal cosmic rule that one must never forget: *rhythm restores power.* This is a basic esoteric principle. Most people today live lives completely devoid of regular rhythm, especially in terms of thinking and behavior. Those who allow the distractions of the outer world to take hold cannot avoid the dangers that the physical body would be exposed to during esoteric development because the forces of renewal are withdrawn. Consequently, we must work to introduce a rhythmic element into life. Naturally, we cannot arrange our days so that each day is exactly like every other. But at least we can pursue some activities regularly. Indeed, this is necessary for anyone who wants to develop on the esoteric path. For example, we should do certain meditation and concentration exercises at a deliberate time every morning. We can also bring rhythm into our lives if in the evening we review the events of the day in reverse order. The more regularities we can introduce, so much the better. In this way, life exists in harmony with the laws of the world. Everything in the system of nature is rhythmic—the course of the Sun, the passing of the seasons, the cycle of day and night, and so on. Plants, too, grow rhythmically. True, the higher we go in the kingdoms of nature, the less rhythm we find, but even in animals we can observe a certain rhythm: for example, they mate at regular times. Only human beings lead a chaotic life without rhythm; nature has deserted it.

Our task, therefore, is to deliberately infuse some rhythm into this chaotic life. And we have certain means available to us through which we can bring harmony and rhythm into our physical and etheric bodies. Both bodies then gradually develop rhythms that will self-regulate when the astral body withdraws. When they are forced out of their proper rhythm during the day, they will, on their own, regain the right kind of movement while at rest.

The means available consist of the following exercises. These practices must be done in addition to meditation:

1. *Thought control.* This means that, at least for a short time every day, you stop all sorts of thoughts from drifting through your mind; for a space of time you allow peace and tranquillity to enter your thinking. You think a definite idea; place it in the center of your thinking; then you logically arrange your thoughts so that they are all closely related to the original idea. Even if you do this for only a minute, it can be very important for the rhythm of the physical and etheric bodies.

2. *Initiative in action.* You must accomplish some act, however trivial, that owes its origin to your own initiative; this is some task you have given yourself. Most actions are a response to your family circumstances, your education, your vocation, and so on. Consider how little arises from your own initiative. Consequently, you must spend a little time performing acts that derive only from yourself. They need not be important; very insignificant actions fulfil the same purpose.

3. *Detachment, imperturbability.* You must learn to regulate your emotions so that you are not one moment up in the sky and

the next down in the dumps. Those who refuse to do this for fear of losing their unconventionality or their artistic sensibility can never develop esoterically. Detachment, or imperturbability, means that you master yourself through the greatest joy and the deepest grief. Indeed, we become truly receptive to the world's joys and sorrows only when we do not enter them egoistically. The greatest artists owe their great achievements precisely to this detachment, because, through it, they have opened their eyes to subtle and inwardly significant impressions.

4. *Impartiality or freedom from prejudice.* This quality sees good in everything and looks for the positive element everywhere. For example, the following Persian legend is told of Christ Jesus. One day Christ Jesus saw a dead dog lying by the wayside; he stopped to look at the animal while those around him turned away in disgust. Then Jesus said: "What beautiful teeth the dog has!" In that hideous corpse he saw, not what was ugly or evil, but the beauty of the white teeth. If you can acquire this mood, you will look everywhere for the good and the positive—and you will find it everywhere. This has a powerful effect on the physical and etheric bodies.

5. *Faith.* In the esoteric sense, faith implies something rather different than its ordinary meaning. During esoteric development, you must never allow your judgment of the future to be influenced by the past. In esoteric development you must exclude all that you have experienced thus far, so that you can meet each new experience with new faith. The esotericist must do this quite consciously. For instance, if someone were to come up to you and say that the church steeple is leaning at a forty-five degree angle, most people would say that that is impossible. Esotericists must always leave a way open for belief. They must go so far as to have faith in everything that happens in the world; otherwise their way to new experiences is barred. You must always remain open to new experiences. In this way, your physical and etheric bodies will assume a condition that may be likened to the contented mood of a setting hen.

6. *Inner Balance*. Inner balance is a natural result of the other five qualities; it is gradually formed from the other five qualities. You must keep these six qualities in mind, grasp life, and advance gradually—like the proverb about drops of water wearing away a stone.

If one acquires higher powers through the artificial means of magic without applying all this, it will lead to no good. In ordinary life, the spiritual and the physical intermingle, somewhat like a blue and yellow liquid in a glass of water. Esoteric development sets in motion a process something like the work of a chemist who separates the two liquids. Similarly, soul and body are separated, and the benefits of the mingling are lost. Ordinary people are not subjected to the more extreme passions because the soul remains in close relation to the body. But as a result of the separation I have been speaking of, the physical body, with all its attributes, may be left to itself, and this can lead to all sorts of excesses. Consequently, those who have embarked on esoteric development, but who have not taken care to cultivate moral qualities, may manifest certain traits that, as ordinary people, they had long ago ceased to manifest. They may suddenly begin to lie, become vengeful or quick to anger—all sorts of characteristics that had previously been toned down may appear in a violent form. This can also happen to those who have neglected moral development and become unduly absorbed in the teachings of spiritual science.

The Three Ways

1. *The Eastern way of development* (also called *yoga*). Here an initiated human being living on the physical plane acts as the guru for another human being, who entrusts himself or herself—completely and in all details—to that guru. This method works best for those who, during esoteric development, entirely eliminate their own self and hand it over to the guru. The guru must advise students on their every action. This absolute surrender of

one's own self is appropriate for the Indian character, but European culture does not tolerate it.

2. *The Christian way of development.* Here, in place of individual gurus, there is one great guru for everyone—the leader of humanity: Jesus Christ himself. The feeling of belonging to Jesus Christ, of being one with him, can replace surrender to an individual guru. But the pupil must first be led to Christ by an earthly teacher; in a certain sense, one still depends on a guru on the physical plane.

3. *The Rosicrucian way of development.* This path leaves the pupil with the greatest possible independence. The guru here is no longer a leader, but an adviser who gives directions for the necessary inner training. At the same time, the guru makes certain that, parallel with the esoteric training, there is a definite development of thinking—without which no esoteric training can be carried through. This is because there is something about thinking that does not apply to anything else. When we are on the physical plane, we perceive with the physical senses only what is on that plane. Astral perceptions are valid for the astral plane; devachanic hearing is valid only in devachan. Thus, each plane has its own specific form of perception. But one activity—logical thinking— goes through all worlds. Logic is the same on all three planes. Thus, on the physical plane you can learn something that is valid also for the higher planes. This is the method followed by Rosicrucian training when, on the physical plane, it gives primary attention to thinking, and for this purpose uses the means available on the physical plane. Penetrative thinking can be cultivated by studying spiritual scientific truths, or by practicing thought exercises. Anyone who wishes further training for the intellect can study books such as *Truth and Science* and *Intuitive Thinking as a Spiritual Path: A Philosophy of Freedom.* They were written deliberately, as a training for thinking, to enable thinking to move with certainty on the highest planes. Even those who study these books while knowing nothing of spiritual science may find their way in the higher worlds. But, as I have said, spiritual scientific teachings

act in the same way as the system of Rosicrucian training: the truest inner guide is one's own clear thinking. Then, a guru will simply be a friend and adviser, since training one's own thinking is training the best guru for oneself. But you will, of course, still need a guru—one to give advice on how to advance independently toward freedom.

Among Europeans, the Christian way is best for those whose *feelings* are most strongly developed. On the other hand, there are those who have broken away somewhat from the Church and rely more on science. Science, however, has led them into a doubting frame of mind. Such people will do best with the Rosicrucian way.

The Christian Way

This Christian way can be followed with the advice of a teacher who knows what has to be done and can rectify mistakes at every step. Keep in mind, however, that in Christian training the great guru is Jesus Christ himself. Hence it is essential to firmly believe in Christ's presence and his life on Earth. Without this, a feeling of union with him is impossible. Furthermore, we must recognize that the Gospel of St. John is a document that originates with the great guru himself and can itself be a source of instruction. This Gospel is something we can experience in our own inner being and not something we merely believe. If you absorb it in the right way you will no longer need to prove the reality of Jesus Christ, for you will have found him.

In Christian training you must meditate on this Gospel, not simply read and reread it. The Gospel begins: "In the beginning was the Word, and the Word was with God, and the Word was God." The opening verses of this Gospel, correctly understood, are sentences for meditation and must be absorbed inwardly in the state of *dhyana* [meditation on concepts that have no sensory perceptible counterpart]. If in the morning, before other impressions have entered the soul, you live for five minutes solely in these sentences, with everything else excluded from your thoughts, and if you continue to do this over the years with absolute patience and perseverance, you will find that these words are not merely something to be understood; you will realize that they have spiritual power, and through them you will indeed experience a transformation of the soul. In a certain sense, you become clairvoyant through these words, so that everything in St. John's Gospel can be seen with astral vision.

Then, under the direction of a teacher, and after meditating again on the five opening verses, you allow the first chapter to pass through your mind for seven days. During the following week, after again meditating on the five opening verses, you go on to the second chapter, and in the same way continue to the twelfth chapter. You will soon realize the power of this experience; you are led into the events in Palestine (as they are inscribed in the akashic record) when Jesus Christ lived there, and you realize that you can actually experience it all. And when you reach the thirteenth chapter, you have to experience the separate stages of Christian initiation.

The first stage is *Washing the Feet*. We must understand the significance of this great scene. Jesus Christ bends down before those who are lower than himself. This humility toward those who are lower than we are, and at whose expense we have been able to rise, must be present everywhere in the world. If a plant were able to think, it would thank the minerals for giving it the ground on which it can lead a higher form of life; the animal would have to bow down before the plant and say, "I owe to you the possibility of my very existence." Likewise, we should recognize what we owe to the rest of nature. So, too, in our society, a person in a higher position should bow before those who are lower and say, "Without the diligence of those who labor on my behalf, I would not be in my present position." And so on through all stages of human existence up to Jesus Christ himself, who bows in meekness before the apostles and says, "You are my ground, and to you I fulfil the saying, 'One who would be first must be last, and the one who would be Lord must be the servant of all.'" Washing the Feet indicates this willingness to serve, this bowing down in perfect humility. Everyone committed to esoteric development must have this feeling.

Those permeated with this humility will have experienced the first stage of Christian initiation. Two signs—an inner and an outer—will let you know when you have done so. The outer sign is your feeling as though your feet were being enthused with water. The inner sign is an astral vision that will come quite certainly—you see yourself washing the feet of a number of persons. This picture arises in dreams as an astral vision, and every student has this same vision. When you have experienced it, you will have truly absorbed this whole chapter.

The second stage is that of the *Scourging*. When you have reached this point, you must, while reading of the Scourging and allowing it to affect you, develop another feeling. You must learn to stand firm under the heavy strokes of life, saying to yourself, "I will stand up to whatever pains and sorrows come my way." The outer sign is that you feel a kind of prickling pain all over your body. The inner sign is a dream vision of seeing yourself being scourged.

The third stage is that of the *Crowning with Thorns*. For this, you must acquire yet another feeling: you learn to stand firm even when you are scorned and ridiculed because of all that you hold most sacred. The outer sign of this is the experience of a severe headache; the inner symptom is that you have an astral vision of yourself being crowned with thorns.

The fourth stage is that of the *Crucifixion*. A new and very definite feeling must now be developed. You must no longer regard your body as the most important thing to you; you must become as indifferent to your body as you would be to a piece of wood. Then you come to an objective view of the body you carry through life; your body becomes for you the wood of the Cross. You need not despise it any more than you would any other tool. The outer sign for having reached this stage is that, during meditation, something like red stigmata appear precisely at those places on the body called the "sacred wounds." They actually appear on the hands and feet, and on the right side of the body at the level of the heart. The inward sign is that you have a vision of yourself hanging on the Cross.

The fifth stage is that of the *Mystical Death*. Now the student experiences the nothingness of earthly things, and indeed dies for a while to all earthly things.

Only the scantiest descriptions can be given of these later stages of Christian initiation. The student experiences in an astral vision that darkness reigns everywhere and that the earthly world has fallen away. A black veil spreads over what is to come. While in this condition, the student comes to know all that exists as evil and wickedness in the world. This is the *Descent into Hell*. Then you experience the tearing away of the curtain and the world of devachan appears before you; this is the *Rending of the Veil* of the Temple.

The sixth stage is that of the *Burial*. Just as at the fourth stage you learned to regard your own body objectively, so now you must develop the feeling that everything else around you in the world is as much part of what truly belongs to you as your own body. The body extends far beyond its skin; you are no longer a separate being; you are united with the whole planet. The Earth has become your body; you are buried in the Earth.

The seventh stage, the *Resurrection*, cannot be described in words. Therefore, esotericism teaches that the seventh stage can be conceived only by a person whose soul has been entirely freed from the brain; it can be described only to those who have achieved this. Consequently, I can do no more than mention it here. The Christian teacher indicates the way to this experience.

When someone has lived through this seventh stage, Christianity will have become an inner experience of the soul. And that person is now wholly united with Jesus Christ; Jesus Christ is in that individual.

5. How Does the Soul Find Its True Being?

Kassel

MAY 8, 1914

How does the soul find its true being? Fundamentally, this is a question that each soul continually asks itself. We need not even phrase the question in such explicit terms, but undoubtedly we can sense in our deepest feelings, in the depths of our soul, that the most profound destiny of the human soul must have something to do with this question. Neither do we need to ponder the usefulness of answering this question, the meaning or scientific value of the answer, and the like. We can feel that our inner peace and balance depend on the ability to at least sense that this question can indeed be answered. Today we will discuss the question from the perspective of the spiritual science that is now accessible to searching human souls.

In the true sense of the word, what spiritual science has to say about this question is a product or result of current human striving and will become ever more so as humanity evolves. In its evolution, humanity passes through various stages, through various peoples and epochs. The natural sciences that are so highly prized today—and rightly so—first entered human evolution at a certain point in time. The same is true of the spiritual science we will speak of here. According to the views and insights of spiritual researchers, the circumstances that permitted the development of the natural sciences three or four centuries ago are now present with regard to spiritual science.

That we are discussing this matter tonight from the perspective of spiritual science, however, does not imply that spiritual science has anything new to say on the subject. On the contrary, what spiritual science says has always been alive in human souls—in general somewhat dimly, but with some degree of clarity in the most influential souls. Let me read a statement by one of the outstanding thinkers in recent intellectual history, a statement that will lead us directly to tonight's question. The great philosopher Johann Gottlieb Fichte once said of individual human destiny: I do not need to be torn out of the context of earthly life in order to gain access to the supraearthly realm. Rather, I am in it now; I live in it now in a much truer sense than I live in the earthly realm. Even now, it is my only secure vantage point, and the life that I have possessed eternally is the only reason I may continue my earthly life. What they call heaven does not lie on the other side of the grave. It is already here; it is spread out all around our nature, and its light dawns in every pure heart.[1]

Although this statement was made by a deeply spiritual person, it was still not possible to speak from the perspective of spiritual science as it is today. At that time the human soul's needs with regard to supraearthly life were not yet as pronounced as they are today. Only the most shortsighted will disagree that, from now on, all thoughtful souls will be increasingly concerned

---

1. Johann Gottlieb Fichte (1762–1814), German philosopher of transcendental idealism emphasizing the self-activity of reason. He attempted to perfect the work of Kant, who influenced Fichte to write *Study for a Critique of All Revelation.* He lectured at Jena, Berlin, and Erlangen, and became Rector at the University of Berlin. Steiner based his doctoral thesis on Fichte's scientific teaching.

by the disharmony they sense between their belief that the soul's real home is what we call the spiritual world (a thought that must begin to dawn in every loving heart) and the fact that our esteemed science (claimed by our best contemporaries to be the only legitimate way to determine the truth) either turns its back on any research into the suprasensory world or, at best, reserves the right to say that our human capacity for knowledge is far too limited to enter that world and, consequently, all information about it is uncertain.

The time is passed when souls did not feel the disharmony between the heart's inner certainty about its suprasensory home and the insistence of science that we are completely unable to know that home. For this very reason, modern spiritual science senses the potential inherent in the human forces cultivated through centuries of researching natural phenomena, and recognizes that those forces must now find their place in our culture as a whole. If used correctly, these forces make it truly possible for us to gain access to spiritual worlds, just as outer cognition, which is bound by the senses and the brain, grants us access to the natural world. Admittedly, this statement still encounters opposition and misunderstandings. When we speak of spiritual science in the sense intended here, we are forced to use very unfamiliar concepts. Consequently, it is quite understandable, even to those of us who are intimately involved with spiritual science, that countless people believe they are standing on firm footing in the scientific school of thought yet continue to reject spiritual science. Fundamentally, however, a drastic change had to occur in people's thought habits three or four centuries ago when the natural sciences initiated a completely different way of thinking about space; similarly, a drastic change in thought habits will also have to take place in human souls in order to permit the spread of an ever-growing understanding of the truths I am outlining in this lecture.

It may be true that spiritual science is the offspring of natural science, but one must also acknowledge that it is possible today for those of us grounded in spiritual science to believe that we have been abandoned by all the good spirits of natural science and by true science altogether. This is because the soul attitude of the spiritual researcher is fundamentally different from that of the natural scientist. Consider the attitude with which natural scientists approach outer nature. They direct their senses—whether unaided or aided by the appropriate instruments—toward external things, and their thinking is applied to recognize the laws governing natural phenomena. When we attempt to understand nature, we confront the world as we naturally are, as we have been placed into the natural world. We apply our natural senses, thinking abilities, and powers of judgment to discovering the facts of existence. We must proceed very differently when we want to gain access to the spiritual world. For this reason, I will now begin to describe the attitude that characterizes the spiritual researcher.

Spiritual researchers do not directly use the senses, powers of judgment, or ordinary cognitive abilities used by natural scientists to approach external objects and human beings. They do, however, use all such faculties in preparing for spiritual research. This preparation is soul work, and all the clarity of thinking, feeling, and perceiving that spiritual scientists can muster is used to develop their souls, which are gradually transformed into different beings, mature enough for what they choose to undertake. When we approach soul development in the way that will be described shortly, our feelings are very different from those with which we approach everyday life. When we honestly conduct spiritual research, we sense reverence and awe for the truth growing in our souls. We feel as if the truth were hovering above us in the distance and that we must first draw near to it. The farther we advance in spiritual research, the more this mood intensifies, and the more we develop the feeling that we must wait. In our present soul condition, we are not yet entitled to approach certain questions about spiritual life. It is as if we were being told to continue to work on our souls until we reach a point of greater maturity, when the questions we would like to have answered today will be answered. Willingness to wait in holy awe to see what the soul achieves, and even to refrain from approaching certain questions about the foundations of existence, is the fundamental attitude required for spiritual research. Spiritual researchers submit to the flow of existence, trusting that wisdom will prevail and that this streaming wisdom will make them ever more ready and mature.

I hope these words have given you a preliminary impression of the attitude that is all-important for spiritual researchers. For them, a great deal depends on being able to stand in holy awe of the truth and on feeling that they must continue to mature before they can approach it. They feel the inner need to subordinate all of their soul efforts to an attitude such as I have just characterized. I do not mean that this attitude must be brought about artificially or that it is imposed on those who want to become spiritual researchers. No, it arises by itself when we do what is necessary for the human soul to discover its true being. But how is this done? Tonight I can point only briefly to the general principles, but you can find a thorough discussion of the details in my books *How to Know Higher Worlds* and *An Outline of Esoteric Science* (part 2). Some very specific details are also in one of my most recent books, *The Threshold of the Spiritual World*.[2]

It would be easy to think that we must practice highly specific and wondrous routines in order to gain access to the spiritual world. This is not so. Basically, all the faculties the soul needs for access to the spiritual world are already present in the life of each human soul, although they are insufficient and mixed in with everything else we experience in our ordinary existence. They exist between the lines of life, as it were. Spiritual researchers must develop them to a level of unlimited strength. One such faculty, which is initially quite inconspicuous in our soul life, is what we ordinarily call "paying attention." We know that we must develop the ability to pay attention even in everyday life. We must be interested in each object and event we encounter. We cannot allow life to simply flood our senses and our intellect; we must

---

2. Contained in *A Way of Self-Knowledge.* See bibliography.

select individual phenomena and beings and pay particular attention to them. This attentiveness, which we develop involuntarily, is our only means of shaping and ordering our soul life.

Before I begin to discuss its application to spiritual research, I would like to demonstrate two ways in which inner attentiveness is already significant in everyday life. A certain philosopher said, and rightly so, that "the question of memory, the capacity to remember, is actually a matter of the human soul's attentiveness." The issues and principles of education can gain a great deal by truly acknowledging what spiritual science has to say about the connection between attention and memory. How many people complain of poor memory, especially as they grow older? Almost all of us, we might say. If we looked at the connection between attention and memory soon enough, this would not be such a problem. We can tell people that the more they make an effort to develop their ability to pay attention—that is, their ability to focus their interest on individual phenomena— and the more they apply inner exertion to concentrating their attention, the stronger their memory and powers of recollection will become. This is not simply because we recall something more easily when we have paid attention to it. Rather, our ability to remember becomes stronger the more we are trained (or train ourselves) to develop the activity of paying attention; the activity and the ability go hand in hand. Not only is it easier to remember something we have paid attention to (as experience readily confirms), but our ability to remember is also strengthened by cultivating the activity of paying attention.

This is one of the ways in which inner attentiveness is significant in everyday life. The second can lead us into a sad chapter in the life of the human soul. I am sure that many of you have heard about extreme instances of amnesia when the life of a human soul is disrupted by the inability to recollect its own experiences. It sometimes happens that people suddenly feel torn away from what they were doing; they no longer realize what they are doing and have forgotten part or all of their earlier soul life. They live as if in a different state of consciousness. They may travel or do any number of things, but their undisturbed, coherent recollection of these experiences reappears only later. Having previously forgotten their I, they very suddenly again become aware of who they are. Such extreme cases constitute an illness, but the human soul's ability to remember is disturbed relatively easily. Such instances would occur much less frequently if we considered that continuity of consciousness—our overview of our own experience, or our intense self-awareness—depends on developing the highest degree of attention. For the sake of their later years, it is very good to encourage children to concentrate their interest on individual beings and processes. Paying attention strengthens both their will—to the extent that will is strengthened by coherent life experience—and their powers of judgment. If we look at our ordinary soul life, however, we are forced to say that paying attention occurs between the lines.

Spiritual researchers or aspiring spiritual researchers must infinitely enhance their ability to pay attention. Ordinarily, only outer causes lead us to take an interest in one thing or another, but spiritual researchers must develop inner skills of concentration. By strongly activating their inner soul forces, they must voluntarily concentrate the soul's entire content and focus it on a mental image not imposed from outside—either an image they themselves construct in their souls or one recommended by expert spiritual researchers. They voluntarily cause such mental images to arise in their souls at certain moments, while simultaneously striving for a state of consciousness in which ordinary thinking ceases and their outer senses perceive nothing. This state of consciousness outwardly resembles sleep, but, in fact, the soul and all its forces are concentrated on a single mental image that is retained for as long as possible. This is known as concentration. You can look up the details in the books I mentioned earlier. The best mental images to place in the center of one's consciousness are symbolic images that are not modeled on anything in the outer world.

It is important for spiritual researchers to repeat this exercise over and over. Depending on their abilities, some people will achieve results after a short time, whereas others may require years of effort. But regardless of how long it takes, humanity's current stage of evolution makes it possible for anyone who makes the effort to achieve this capacity for soul enhancement. Patient and persistent practice of such concentration exercises brings to the surface forces that otherwise lie dormant, as if in the soul's depths. We do not become spiritual researchers in an outer, tumultuous way. We do it by infinitely enhancing soul processes such as paying attention. When this enhancement has occurred, and at the appropriate point in time, what might be called a spiritual chemical process takes place. Let me emphasize that this term in and of itself does not prove anything, so please do not place any particular value on it. As I describe this process, you will see that our modern spiritual science seeks the true being of the human soul in ways that are similar—but only similar—to how the natural sciences attempt to hear the secrets of nature. Because spiritual science enters the domain of the spirit, its methods of research and preparation must be different from those of the natural sciences.

The concept of spiritual chemistry can help make the matter understandable by analogy: We cannot see hydrogen in water; therefore, we cannot tell by looking at water that chemists can separate hydrogen out of it. Water puts out fire, but hydrogen burns. It is impossible to see the essential properties of hydrogen by looking at water; similarly, it is impossible to see the soul nature of a person by looking at that person's body. Chemists can extract hydrogen from water, although its properties are totally different from those of water; similarly, spiritual researchers, by using their own souls as instruments of research, can separate their souls from their bodies during concentration. The spiritual and soul aspect of a spiritual researcher separates from the physical, bodily aspect. The abstract, monistic, natural scientific world view, which ignores the facts, will call our view "dualism," but we might as well speak of the dualism of water. Water, too, is not simply a monolithic unity, and in order to understand it completely we must extract hydrogen from it. Just as hydrogen can be extracted from water through a physical-chemical process, the spirit and soul can be separated from the physical body through processes such as the one I just described. You will find descriptions of other such processes in the books I mentioned. Spiritual researchers experience a great and significant event when they truly make sense of the statement, "I experience myself as a being of soul and spirit independent and outside of my body." This statement makes no sense to those who know nothing about the phenomena of spiritual experience. And since I do not want to speak in abstract terms about the phenomena involved in discovering the soul's true being, I will not hesitate to describe some of the experiences of spiritual researchers.

Standing in the midst of ordinary life, where the soul and spirit are bound to the body just as the hydrogen in water is bound to oxygen, we look at the world knowing that our bodily instruments develop our soul powers. That is, we make use of our senses and our brain; we live within the body. We may call the power of thinking the first faculty to alert us to the fact that our soul and spirit are dwelling outside the body after we have done the exercises described. In ordinary life, we know that this power of thinking is usable because it is bound to the brain. Now, however, we experience ourselves in our thoughts as existing and moving around outside of the brain. This is no fairy tale or hypothesis; you can experience it yourself by practicing the appropriate exercises. You will come to realize that you are now dwelling within your thought life as if it were floating outside of your own brain; in other words, your powers of thinking are developing outside your body.

When this happens, there is one almost shattering moment that we experience with particularly intensity. After we have made the effort to do these exercises for some time, but still cannot quite experience thinking outside of the brain and concentration still results in a dreamlike twilight, a moment will come when we are clearly aware for the first time of plunging back down into the brain, of making the transition from the thinking that takes place outside of the body to thinking within the body. We sense that the being we experienced outside of the body is plunging back down into something difficult to penetrate. It is as if soothing currents surround us as our thinking being moves back into the body, penetrating the brain in order to use it for outer thinking once again.

Given the nature of these phenomena, it is quite understandable that so many people today would say that this is all nonsense, the fantasies of a half-crazed mind. Nonetheless, these are the phenomena that will teach people to recognize the soul's true being. Such phenomena will become prevalent in the culture of the future, because people's souls are hungering for them, although unconsciously as yet. These phenomena will pervade our culture as surely as did the Copernican view of Earth moving at high speed through space.

As we have seen, the power of thinking is the first faculty that can be separated from the physical body. Emancipating thinking from its physical organs is generally the first suprasensory experience we can have if we have the stamina to carry out the above-mentioned exercises for a longer period of time. In order to have such experiences, we must simply overcome certain individual obstacles. For example, those who are interested only in physical existence and are unable to develop altruistic interests will encounter great obstacles when they make this attempt. Their souls must first acquire altruistic interests—that is, the ability to notice the beauty and nobility displayed by each and every being, even in the physical world. People who are interested only in themselves and whose ordinary thinking is limited to egotistical concerns will soon notice that, although they progress through the exercises described, their souls are overcome by a certain inner fear of the world they intended to enter, the world experienced outside of the body. Essentially, this fear is always present in the soul, but we remain unaware of it. In spiritual science, we speak of the threshold between the sensory and the spiritual worlds, the earthly and the supraearthly. We say that we must cross this threshold. We even say that a guardian watches over it, meaning, of course, a spiritual power. But if it is true—and spiritual science confirms that it is—that the spiritual world is all around us, as Fichte says, and that we are capable of finding our way into it, why isn't it as apparent to the human soul as the physical world? Because aspiring spiritual researchers have experiences (such as those just described) that cause fear to appear in their souls as an effective antidote to premature entry into the spiritual world. This fear is always present in human souls but is not evident as such. It becomes apparent when people falter in their efforts to reach the spiritual world. Such people seem to become nonchalant and uninterested in continuing their exercises, and the reason is fear, fear that is not felt because it is not perceived as fear.

We can even say that spiritual research reveals the source of humanity's materialistic attitude. In this day and age, there are indeed materialistically-minded souls who say either that it is impossible for us to speak of a spiritual world or that we should not worry about that world because our human capacity for knowledge is restricted to the sensory world. They also say that it is unscientific to speak of a life in the spirit. Nowadays such people go by the genteel name of monists; we used to simply call them materialists. They deem themselves especially scientific when they completely deny the existence of a spiritual world or say that science has nothing to do with that world. Of course, when we state the truth about spiritual phenomena, we can scarcely expect to find support among dyed-in-the-wool monists. This truth remains the truth, however, and it is fear, rather than any logical reasons or proof, that keeps souls imprisoned in materialism or monism. People do not recognize this fear as such and do not acknowledge it to themselves. Nonetheless, fear gives rise to the idea that it is unscientific to investigate the spiritual world. Anyone who understands the factors involved knows that materialistic organizations attract souls dominated by fear of the spiritual world. It is not pleasant to tell people that they are basically fearful souls and that they are simply cloaking their fear in a semblance of logic, as if they could prove that only the phenomena of the physical world are entitled to exist.

We have now pointed out the obstacles that prevent the soul from entering the spiritual world to which its true being belongs.

Next, other exercises must be added to the ones described. These new exercises are done alternately; they must be performed in such a way that the soul does not link one to the other. Just as a pendulum swings from one side to the other and cannot swing in both directions at once, the soul cannot perform different exercises at the same time; one should do them in alternation so that they support each other. We have talked about how to heighten our attentiveness. Similarly, we can also infinitely enhance another quality that exists between the lines in ordinary life, namely, what we know as devotion—the devotion we experience when something lays claim to us so completely that we forget everything else around us and dwell only on what commands this devotion. We must submit passively to devotion, whereas paying attention requires activity. Such devotion must become universal, so to speak, if we want to become spiritual researchers. As it develops, we again cultivate a soul attitude that looks like sleep but is in fact its opposite. The will must totally come to rest, even the will that is expressed in the tiniest motion of our limbs. All arbitrary thinking and all perception must come to rest, but the soul is awake and submits fully to the stream of existence while cultivating this attitude in the absolute stillness that religious people may experience when they are truly inwardly devout in their prayers. But in spiritual research, we do not give ourselves up even to the content of a prayer, which would put the soul in a particular mood. With our entire being, we surrender only to the eternal power of existence. In the soul, this surrender has the effect of bringing up forces that are different from the mere power of thinking.

I would now like to characterize a second force that is embedded in our soul experience and can be brought up in this way. As I tell you this, I am choosing my words on the basis of thoughts that are played out in my brain and take hold of my speech organs. I am making use of physical organs to express what I want to say to you. Just as concentration emancipates our powers of thinking from the physical organ of the brain, the force that ordinarily flows into our speech organs can be separated both from these organs and from the brain. Although this force is then outwardly totally mute, we cultivate it on a soul level. The unexpressed inner word becomes active when what ordinarily flows out into speech is retained in the soul and developed internally. This word cannot be heard with any physical organ; we each hear it inwardly when we listen to our own Self. What we might call the spiritual outer world streams into this spiritual word, which resounds all the more clearly because it is mute, and which we gain by emancipating our powers of speech from their physical organs.

In the physical world, we are surrounded by beings of the mineral, plant, animal, and human kingdoms. Similarly, when we release our powers of thinking and speech from the body and make use of an inner, soul-spiritual mode of experiencing our surroundings, we enter a world where we are surrounded by spiritual beings, forces, and processes. Today it is still somewhat unforgivable to speak about this world. Some philosophers take the liberty of speaking about a spiritual world in general terms, because they have seen the absurdity of denying that such a world exists, but they say nothing more than that a spiritual world exists behind the sensory world. Certain thinkers imagine themselves to be very advanced because they subscribe to a so-called pantheistic view. If you really understand what is at stake, their approach is no better than that of a pan-naturalist who walks across a blooming meadow saying, "What do I care about red or yellow flowers, about these mountains and valleys and rivers—it's all just nature, nature, nature. I'm not interested in the individual physical phenomena that can be observed." Those who permit us to speak of spirit only in the pantheistic sense relate to the spiritual world like a pan-naturalist who dismisses everything as "nature."

Real spiritual research takes a different approach by considering the soul-spiritual aspect of the human being and the physical body as truly separate, thus revealing that the soul-spiritual aspect is as different from the living physical body as hydrogen is from water. Spiritual science enters the spiritual world in a way that makes it possible to distinguish concrete individual beings and events there. Through such spiritual research, we confront the spiritual world in the same way that we human beings in the physical world research the mineral, plant, animal, and human kingdoms. When we look at the physical world, we are on its highest level, but when we look at the spiritual world, we are on its lowest level. As our souls begin to find their place as spiritual beings in the spiritual world, we see above us the hierarchy of superordinate spirits. We ascend to the ranks of spiritual beings to which our soul-spiritual aspect belongs just as the physical human body belongs to the physical, mineral kingdom. We accomplish this by emancipating our powers of speech, by retaining within us what otherwise unites with the body by streaming out into the bodily organs of speech.

We can expand upon this experience by retaining the inner faculty we know in everyday life as memory. Memory appears in the soul when we review the events of our life as far back as we can remember. These events rise from the soul's depths as images and thoughts of things past. When the soul progresses in the way just described, a time comes when the images that rise out of the soul's indistinct depths no longer express what we have experienced in this lifetime. Instead, they lead us out of this world into a purely spiritual world. The soul-power of memory expands to such an extent that we really experience the meaning of these words: "Before I was born or conceived in physical matter by my parents, I existed in a spiritual world where I had certain experiences; earlier still, I experienced going back into previous earthly lives. When I step through the portal of death, I will again enter a spiritual world. What I develop within myself in this life is the seed of earthly lives to come. I will experience these future lives with the same degree of certainty as this present one." The human soul experiences the repetition of earthly lives, and the forms of existence lying between them, as the result of the soul's search for its true being and as an inner, empirical fact.

Our inner experience after releasing our powers of thinking can be compared to an inner play of facial expressions on the soul level. We cannot approach the spiritual world passively, as we do the outer world with our senses. As soon as we realize that we are outside the body with our powers of thinking, we must keep these powers constantly active. This is the difference between spiritual perception and physical perception. Physical perception allows us to think and to surrender to that thinking, but when we enter the spiritual world with our emancipated powers of thinking, we must remain constantly active. We must slip inside or plunge into the spiritual beings we want to perceive. We must be constantly active. If we cease to be active, our spiritual perception also ceases. We can call this perception an inner play of facial expressions. We voluntarily express what our perception is, what we are able to know about the other being. We do this by adapting our own emancipated thinking to the events and beings we perceive.

Similarly, emancipated speech, or dwelling in the inner word, can be called an inner gesture. In outer life, when we are totally caught up in our subject and express our experiences through activity, we gesture—sometimes too much, like me when I lecture. In physical life, our gestures and movements express what is inside us; similarly, as our powers of speech are emancipated and we make the transition into the spiritual world and its events, our inner gestures must express what belongs to the other being. Thus you can see the great difference between true spiritual perception and sensory perception. Sensory perception is passive, but spiritual perception is active.

Continuing with these exercises, we come to another human faculty. To express what I want to clarify, let me refer to child development. As the natural sciences can also explain, when human beings enter physical existence they must first acquire the upright posture they need for life in the outer physical world. Animals enter physical life differently; any claims to the contrary are illusory. Human beings as they first enter life are helpless, crawling creatures who need to acquire uprightness. Important thinkers have always pointed out what it means for human beings to be able to stand upright and look out at the heavens. The forces enabling us to become upright beings develop during childhood, when we give our whole body its outer form. We incorporate spirit into the body provided by heredity, which makes the body upright by means of spiritual forces, not mere physical forces. (This statement can also be proved scientifically, but that would take us too far afield today.) These forces are rooted in the spirit and soul but pervade the body, giving it its upright posture. We incorporate the spiritual aspect into the body during earliest childhood, allowing it to stream into the body so that we can become upright. This spiritual aspect can be emancipated from the body in the same way that we emancipate our powers of thinking and speech. Admittedly, the power that grants us uprightness in childhood is the faculty that is most difficult to emancipate, but we do eventually acquire the ability to extract it from the body, so that we can assume any position at will once we are outside the body.

In particular, we learn the great difference between up and down, which are not spatial directions. The upward direction is an inner experience. Once we have emancipated the power of uprightness from the body, a profound moral experience arises in the soul, outside of the body. This experience resembles a counter-gravitational force, but it is neither directional nor spatial. It can be expressed somewhat as follows. In truly experiencing this "up," the soul feels increasingly lonely; you go through all the moods that result from the impression of being more and more alone. You know that a world exists outside of you and that you can perceive nothing of it on a spiritual level. You disappear as far as this world is concerned; you are increasingly isolated within yourself. If your soul is not attuned to this loneliness in the way you can read about in my book *How to Know Higher Worlds*, this mood of loneliness will come over you and you will sense that an entire world exists within you. You will sense, however, that you yourself are constantly rising while that world sinks away beneath you. This mood, in which the soul senses a whole world within itself, can also be bound up with fear of your own Self, with the fear of experiencing all sorts of tragic and blissful conflicts as you become aware of everything that exists in the depths of a human soul.

Spiritual science is able to ascertain that the human soul lives again and again in moods such as this—alternating with other moods that I will describe shortly—in the purely spiritual world during the time between death and a new birth. In my mystery drama, *The Souls' Awakening*, I referred to the moment midway between death and rebirth as "the cosmic midnight hour of existence," because in the midst of the blissfulness of spiritual life prior to its next birth, the soul actually does experience a moment in which it is totally alone [scene 6]. It experiences only itself and can become very apprehensive in its awareness of the existence of a world that surrounds it but is outside its consciousness, a world of which it knows nothing, a world or worlds that can rise from within the soul itself. The soul is together with these worlds in its loneliness.

Spiritual researchers also become familiar with another mood, which can be described as "down"; here the soul feels as if it were radiating its own soul light outward. In the physical world, we see or perceive objects because the Sun shines on them. Similarly, we must allow the light of the spirit to shine on objects in the spiritual world. Moments of loneliness stream into us when we falter in our efforts to allow the inner sun to shine. When the light of our inner sun shines, we spread ourselves out over the world of other beings, so to speak. We might call this state spiritual companionship, or spiritual togetherness, with souls with whom we once lived who died before or after us. Or these souls may also still be incarnated on Earth, since we can also perceive such souls from the vantage point of the spirit world. This condition of soul-spiritual perception, or living in companionship with others, alternates with the condition of loneliness during the time between death and a new birth. These two conditions alternate regularly, just as day and night do in our physical existence. We acquire the ability to feel both alone (but in possession of an inner world) and poured out over the spiritual world and its beings and events.

We also become familiar with other forces that can be compared to right and left, forward and back. In ordinary life we know nothing about these forces, because they develop in the subconscious as the soul takes on bodily form for this world. Once we have developed all these forces, of which the power of uprightness is an example, we increasingly acquire an ability to live our way into the spiritual world, the world of the spiritual beings that are all around us. We leave our bodies totally when this happens; we see our bodies outside of us, and we are able to enter other spiritual beings and assume their forms. Here on Earth, we must develop our initial physiognomy, our upright stance. In the spiritual world, we must take on the inner form and constitution of spiritual beings. This is how the human soul connects with the world in which its spiritual essence is truly rooted.

Everything I have attempted to describe is really (to use a rather trivial expression) spiritual chemistry of a sort. The soul frees itself from the living body and becomes part of a new compound, just as hydrogen can do when extracted from water. This new compound is the soul's connection to its true home, the world of its actual roots. Of course it can be said that only spiritual researchers can know anything about the spiritual world, and that therefore we must become spiritual researchers if we wish to truly enter that world. But this is not so. It is not necessary to be a painter in order to understand a painting produced by an artist; similarly, it is not necessary to be a spiritual researcher in order to understand the statements of spiritual researchers. As you can deduce from my books, to a certain extent it is possible for any modern person to become a spiritual researcher, but we need not do so. You must be an artist in order to produce paintings, and you must be a spiritual researcher in order to enter the spiritual world. In the physical world, however, it is indeed possible to find the right words to describe what is proclaimed in the spiritual world. The statements of spiritual researchers can be understood by every human soul. And such statements are unlike any other teachings or theories. They have a totally different relationship to our life. This is not simply a matter of not needing to be a chemist in order to understand the processes that chemists investigate in their experiments. It is more like not having to cultivate a crop in order to live off its yields. We need not do all the work of growing food ourselves in order to eat it. Similarly, if what spiritual researchers say is rooted in the truth, it speaks a secret language that is truly accessible to every human soul.

This language is indeed present in every soul. Many people today believe that the statements of spiritual researchers are crazy or absurd. Such people, however, have simply acquired prejudices instead of powers of judgment. Once we finally recognize the true significance of conventional science, these prejudices will disappear and the mysterious forces of understanding already present in the human soul will come to the fore. Spiritual science will be understood because it strikes secret chords that must resound in the human soul, just as inevitably as our taste nerves develop the sensation of taste when food contacts them. The time will come when we no longer speak about spiritual science as we do today. Instead, the words of spiritual teachers will resound and the souls of even non-seers will be receptive to them. Spiritual science will permit us to enjoy the soul's birthright just as we enjoy the fruits of the field without growing them ourselves and eat grain without running the mill. A time will come, though we are still far from it today, when the mysterious language that lives in every soul will be activated; spiritual researchers will no longer preach in the wilderness but will make their listeners realize that their words merely evoke what is already present in all souls.

When this time comes, we will know that a science of the spiritual world exists and that it is as certain as the natural sciences—indeed, much more certain. What Fichte divined will be confirmed in a truly scientific way: we dwell in the spiritual world not only after death, but we can also live in it and understand it here and now, in the physical world. In fact, we live in the spiritual world in a much truer sense than we do in the physical world. We will come to understand that physical existence is given value, certainty, and confirmation by our understanding of how the human soul finds its true being in the spiritual world.

I would like to mention in passing (not as a boast but simply as a fact) that some understanding exists now for the world that spiritual science will reveal to human beings as the divine spiritual world in which our souls have their true roots. The dawning of this understanding is confirmed by the relatively great expenditure of resources now taking place in Dornach, Switzerland (near Basel) in order to erect a permanent home for this science of the spirit. We call it the School of Spiritual Science. The main reason for its construction is our desire for a building whose artistic style and outer forms express what flows into the human soul from divine spiritual life when the soul discovers its true being. This double-domed wooden building is already standing; it simply needs to be completed inside and out. Its artistic form will express the intentions of spiritual science.

A number of friends of spiritual science have pooled their resources to raise the considerable sums needed for the construction of this building, which we hope will not be understood in the same sense as that of a Paris newspaper article that was circulated worldwide. Let us hope that it is understood as the first site dedicated to the science of the spirit, the science of the human soul's divine origins and true being. The insight of spiritual researchers leads them to believe that many souls already long for this science without being aware of it, and that this longing will continue to grow in the future. We can point with a certain satisfaction to the imposing building we have constructed as a material token of the impression spiritual science has made on individual souls, even though we still encounter one misunderstanding after another when we talk about spiritual science.

Let me draw a comparison today with regard to the soul attitude that spiritual researchers maintain, even when they see prejudices mounting against spiritual science. When this happens, they are forced to recall that there was once a time when people looked up as far as their eyes could see and saw the blue dome of the heavens. Trusting their senses, they saw the dome of the heavens with the Moon, the stars, and the Sun making their way across it. Then along came Copernicus and Giordano Bruno, standing alone in front of their contemporaries, telling them that what they thought they saw with their eyes did not exist in space, that the blue dome of heaven was created by their limited vision, that there is no boundary, that the expanses of the universe extend into infinite space and cradle infinite worlds, that the limits of their own knowledge created the firmament.

To people who trusted only their senses, the firmament once appeared to be a real boundary. It was not actually there, but the limits of cognition placed it there. Similarly, spiritual researchers today know that the sense of being locked in between birth and death is a temporal firmament that human beings create for themselves. Just as Giordano Bruno challenged the spatial firmament, modern spiritual research must challenge this temporal firmament of birth (or conception) and death, telling us that behind birth and death lies the spiritual world, where life extends over all time, cradled in endless repetitions of earthly lives stretching forward and backward like the unending worlds Giordano Bruno once pointed to. We have become accustomed to no longer seeing the spatial firmament as a boundary; just as certainly, we will come to view entering and leaving the body as a temporal firmament beyond which lies the spiritual world, where we dwell with the forces that spiritual science reveals to us.

I have pointed out that when we free the soul from the body through concentration and meditation, we experience what may be called an inner play of expressions, inner gesturing, or inner physiognomy. Even in our present existence, we experience what surrounds the soul completely in the spiritual world after death.

Knowledge of the spiritual world projects into our earthly world, and the soul comes to know itself by discovering its true being, which is rooted in the spiritual world. Understandably enough, such views are not well received at present. What do most people look at today? Let me use a trivial example. A poster advertises a lecture with slides. A poster right next to it advertises a lecture without slides. Which lecture are people most attracted to? To the one where they do not have to be active, of course, where everything is presented to them in pretty pictures. Spiritual science cannot proceed in this way. Although it would also be possible to present what is seen in the spirit in pictures, I have attempted to work only through the medium of the word, which can affect people's thinking and feeling. Spiritual science needs to be able to count on active soul participation.

Recently we were forced to experience an article in an important weekly paper. It said, more or less, that many of our contemporaries find that when they read Spinoza and Kant, the concepts get so confused that they cannot cope with them. But then the author of that article suggests applying a new technical accomplishment to this problem, too. Let's make a film! Imagine a film in which Spinoza first explains how he grinds lenses and then goes on to explain the development of his thoughts and philosophy, and so forth. All you need to do is sit passively, and your thoughts on the subject will no longer be confused. This is totally in line with current preferences. Slide presentations would show us how Spinoza's *Ethics* and Kant's *Critique of Pure Reason* came about. People would go to lectures like that.[3]

We can say, therefore, that in this day and age we are indolent enough to passively allow everything to influence us. Spiritual science, however, demands just the opposite. Human souls must

3. Baruch Spinoza (1632–1677), Dutch philosopher and theologian whose controversial pantheistic doctrine advocated an intellectual love of God. Immanuel Kant (1724–1804), German idealist philosopher who argued that reason is the means by which the phenomena of experience are translated into understanding.

actively acquire spiritual science in order to receive what is most necessary for a healthy soul and spirit: activity, will-strengthening, and strengthening our powers of thinking and feeling. We also need strengthening from another source. When you enter the world of loneliness through your own efforts, you encounter great obstacles. Any unloving feeling you have ever harbored toward any person or animal acts as a barrier. Therefore, when very unloving people cultivate what I called the forces of uprightness, they are stopped short by their own lack of love, which surrounds them on all sides like an outer world. Thus spiritual science urges people to increasingly develop the most profound, enlivened force of love. Those who recognize that life in the future will require love above all else will also know the significance of spiritual science for life both now and in the future. They will also know that the soul's means of finding its true being lies in strengthening the forces of love, because lack of love erects barriers in the spiritual world.

On the one hand, it is evident everywhere that human souls still resist spiritual science because it places demands on as yet unfamiliar habits of thought. On the other hand, souls hunger more or less unconsciously for spiritual science. Here we encounter something that is often stated but needs to be understood correctly. Our time has been called a period of transition. What it has been called, however, is not the point; the question is, a transition to what? Where should our age be going? Our passive submission to a purely sensory based science, where the soul cannot find its true being, must make the transition to spiritual science, where it can.

We must become aware of the image that begins the Western world's main religious document. (There is no need to discuss this image in detail. You can interpret it as you will, but everyone knows that it has to do with good and evil.) There we find the words, "Ye shall be as gods, knowing good and evil."[4] Whether we

---

4. Genesis 3:5, King James version.

take this symbolically or in some other sense, there can be no doubt that the meaning of these words has to do with human freedom and with arrogance, presumption, and the human fall into evil. I do not want to discuss this at greater length today, but we live in an age—if I may offer a somewhat radical characterization of modern life—when we hear a similar whispered word of temptation. When we consider what results when sensory based science is misunderstood (not when it is understood correctly), we need only describe how so many people today believe that human beings with all their faculties, including those of soul and spirit, are nothing more than a higher product of animal evolution. Many people are proud of saying that the qualities present in humans are present in the animal kingdom as well, that morality is simply a higher development of animal instincts. This worldview has a specific consequence, an obvious conclusion that people fail to draw. As a result, they also fail to notice that if natural science really did teach the view just stated—that human beings evolved from animals and that their possession of morality does not originate in a totally different world—then what we hear (if we know how to listen to the voices of our time), as if whispered by a new tempter, would have to be true. We can deny the existence of this new tempter, because "little folk never hear the devil, even when he has them by the collar!" The whispered words we hear are, "You will become like the animals, and good and evil will be like natural laws. The Sun shines on good and evil alike, and the same will be true of natural laws. You will no longer be able to distinguish good from evil."

We do not hear these words spoken aloud, because we fail to draw the necessary conclusion. As we see, the opposite of the original temptation stalks our time of transition. Instead of saying, "Ye shall be like gods, knowing good from evil," the tempter now says, "You will become like the animals; like animals, you will do good and evil without knowing the difference."

This is the goal that spiritual science will work toward, regardless of how many opponents it has today: that human souls may know their true nature and not succumb to this temptation—not even in their feelings, not daring to speak it out. People today still harbor many prejudices against spiritual science, but what certainty and inner stillness can provide contains truth that will benefit the continued activity of spiritual science and the human soul's possibility of finding its true being. I will now attempt to condense the entire meaning of what I tried to present to you this evening into a single feeling, in the hope that my concluding words will be clothed in this certainty and stillness with regard to the goals of spiritual science.

Spiritual science, as a true science and as described here, is a product of modern times. Human souls, having passed through earlier earthly lives, are now becoming more and more ready to develop the forces that lead to spiritual research. If we live for this spiritual research, we feel in harmony with what people expressed before spiritual science existed, when the guiding spirits of humanity's evolution spoke through the deepest divinations and most mature aspects of human souls. Let me present two quotations that accord with what has been said here. Feuchtersleben, the physician and psychologist, to whom we owe the book *Soul Dietetics*, coined a wonderfully beautiful phrase that coincides totally with what spiritual science has to say about the soul's search for its true being: "The human soul cannot conceal from itself that its ultimate happiness consists only in expanding its inner being and possessions." Spiritual science attempts to point the human soul in the direction of its own expansion and its possession of a home in the spiritual world.

Whenever the tempter whispers, "You will become like the animals from which you evolved; you will no longer distinguish good and evil but will believe only in natural laws," we can comfort ourselves as spiritual researchers and know that we are in accord with a great mind whose own inklings always expressed harmony with what spiritual science has to offer. In order to confront the new words of the tempter, "You will be like animals, who do not distinguish good from evil," spiritual science engenders thoughts in the human soul that are summed up by Schiller.[5] In the face of this new temptation, spiritual science reinforces Schiller's words and imbues the human soul with them as if with an all-pervasive feeling. Let these words mark the conclusion of what I felt free to say to you tonight:

> Free and beautiful, the soul now turns
> from the senses' sleep;
> Unchained by you, the slave of cares
> now leaps into the womb of joy.
> Animal nature's dull confines fall away.
> Humanity appears upon the brightened brow
> and thought, that exalted stranger,
> springs from astonished brain.
>
> (from "The Artist")

These words of Schiller were prophetic. To them, spiritual science adds that thought not only springs from the divining soul but truly emerges from the soul to experience itself outside the body, guiding the soul to its true being.

Thought sprang from the astonished brain and gave humans their true being and dignity—that is what Schiller said, and this is what spiritual science and the human soul must acknowledge before true self-understanding can occur.

---

5. Johann Christoph Friedrich von Schiller (1759–1805), German poet, dramatist, philosopher, and historian considered the greatest dramatist of the German theater and one of the greatest in European literature. As a student, Schiller wrote poetry and finished his first play, *The Robbers* (1781). Other works include *Intrigue and Love* (1783); *Don Carlos* (1787); *Wallenstein* (1799); *The Maid of Orleans* (1801); *William Tell* (1804). Schiller's plays are characterized by moral idealism, strong optimism, eloquent poetic diction, and a classic sense of form. Among his best-known works are the philosophical *Letters on the Aesthetic Education of Man* (1795) and the much loved poem, "The Song of the Bell" (1800).

Bibliography

The Essentials of Anthroposophic Spiritual Development

Intuitive Thinking As a Spiritual Path: A Philosophy of Freedom (1894), Anthroposophic Press, Hudson, NY, 1995. Rudolf Steiner lays out the prerequisites for a path of brain- and sense-free thinking as well as the epistemological foundations for his spiritual scientific observation. This work is also known as *The Philosophy of Freedom* and *The Philosophy of Spiritual Activity.*

How To Know Higher Worlds: A Modern Path of Initiation (1904), Anthroposophic Press, Hudson, NY, 1994. This is Rudolf Steiner's classic account of the modern path of initiation. He gives precise instructions for spiritual practice and descriptions of its results.

Theosophy: An Introduction to the Spiritual Processes in Human Life and in the Cosmos (1904), Anthroposophic Press, Hudson, NY, 1994. Steiner presents a comprehensive picture of human nature, beginning with the physical body, moving up through the soul to our spiritual being, with an overview of the laws of reincarnation and the working of karma. He describes a path of knowledge by which we can begin to understand the various ways we live in the worlds of body, soul, and spirit.

An Outline of Esoteric Science (1910), Anthroposophic Press, Hudson, NY, 1998. Originally intended to be a continuation of *Theosophy*, this work deals with the nature and evolution of humanity and the cosmos. It also extends and deepens much of what he describes in *Theosophy*. It contains a description of the path of knowledge, including the "Rose Cross meditation," complementing the descriptions in *Theosophy* and *How to Know Higher Worlds*. Previously titled *An Outline of Occult Science.*

A Way of Self-Knowledge (1912–1913), Anthroposophic Press, Hudson, NY, 1999. This volume begins with *The Threshold of the Spiritual World*, a series of short, aphoristic descriptions of the world and human nature as seen with spiritual vision beyond the boundary between the sensory and spiritual realms. It is intended to present a few descriptions of certain spiritual experiences. From this perspective, these descriptions as well as those in *A Way of Self-Knowledge* should be considered supplementary to the other basic books; nevertheless, these descriptions stand on their own. The eight "meditations" in part two, *A Way of Self-Knowledge*, unfolds in the reader and reveal the hidden inner forces that can be awakened in every soul. Previously titled *A Road to Self-Knowledge*.

Other Works by Rudolf Steiner on Inner Development

Anthroposophical Leading Thoughts: Anthroposophy as a Path of Knowledge, Rudolf Steiner Press, London, 1998.

Anthroposophy in Everyday Life, Anthroposophic Press, Hudson, NY, 1995.

At the Gates of Spiritual Science, Rudolf Steiner Press, London, 1986.

The Effects of Esoteric Development, Anthroposophic Press, Hudson, NY, 1997.

Esoteric Development: Selected Lectures and Writings from the Works of Rudolf Steiner, Anthroposophic Press, Hudson, NY, 1982.

From the History & Contents of the First Section of the Esoteric School, 1904–1914, Anthroposophic Press, Hudson, NY, 1998.

Guidance in Esoteric Training: From the Esoteric School, Rudolf Steiner Press, London, 1994.

The Souls' Awakening: A Mystery Drama, Anthroposophic Press, Hudson, NY, 1995.

The Stages of Higher Knowledge, Anthroposophic Press, Hudson, NY, 1967.

Truth and Knowledge: Introduction to "Philosophy of Spiritual Activity," Garber Communications, Blauvelt, NY, 1981.

Verses and Meditations, Rudolf Steiner Press, London, 1993.

About Rudolf Steiner and Inner Development

Barnes, Henry, *A Life for the Spirit: Rudolf Steiner in the Crosscurrents of Our Time*, Anthroposophic Press, Hudson, NY, 1997.

Childs, Gilbert, *Rudolf Steiner: His Life and Work*, Anthroposophic Press, Hudson, NY, 1996.

Kühlewind, Georg, *Working With Anthroposophy: The Practice of Thinking*, Anthroposophic Press, NY, 1992.

Lievegoed, Bernard, *Man on the Threshold: The Challenge of Inner Development*, Hawthorn Press, Stroud, UK, 1985.

Lowndes, Florin, *Enlivening the Chakra of the Heart: The Fundamental Spiritual Exercises of Rudolf Steiner*, Sophia Books, London, 1998.

McDermott, Robert A., ed., *The Essential Steiner*, Harper Collins, San Francisco, 1984.

During the last two decades of the nineteenth century, the Austrian-born Rudolf Steiner (1861–1925) became a respected and well-published scientific, literary, and philosophical scholar, particularly known for his work on Goethe's scientific writings. After the turn of the century he began to develop his earlier philosophical principles into an approach to methodical research of psychological and spiritual phenomena.

His multifaceted genius has led to innovative and holistic approaches in medicine, philosophy, religion, education (Waldorf schools), special education, economics, science, agriculture (Biodynamic method), architecture, drama, the new arts of speech and eurythmy, and other fields of activity. In 1924 he founded the General Anthroposophical Society, which today has branches throughout the world.